scanning your desires before you even know them

SCHIZOPHRENIC

LODOWN GRAPHIC ENGINEERING PART II
"THE COLOUREXPLOSION"

this book is dedicated to all the creative headz who put all their substance of being in the effort creating
new visual communication skills for our desaturated social outcome at the end of the twenties century
and start processing building new images for the postindustrialized and traumatized human society on
a daily basis.
discover the blueprint of a specific subculture, which is setting their focus in playing with and sampling
urban mechanisms and transforming them to their own art of expression, deeply routed in american popart,
graffitti, electronic music, skateboarding or whatever.
enjoy more than exploit.

analog development meets digital desktop treatment. back in 1998 we made it reproduced.
photography by flach.

MAD FLAVOR
FOR '88

ESCAPE THE CITY LIMITS.

escape the citylimits is my claim, when things get a little bit hectic in an unfriendly urban environment,
breathe life.
terranova sets it up in sound via berlin to the world.
all around the ldwn camp. photocredits to a.d. and alex foley

last.99

PREMILLENNIUM HYSTERIC LODOWN ISSUE NINETEEN IN NINETYNINE

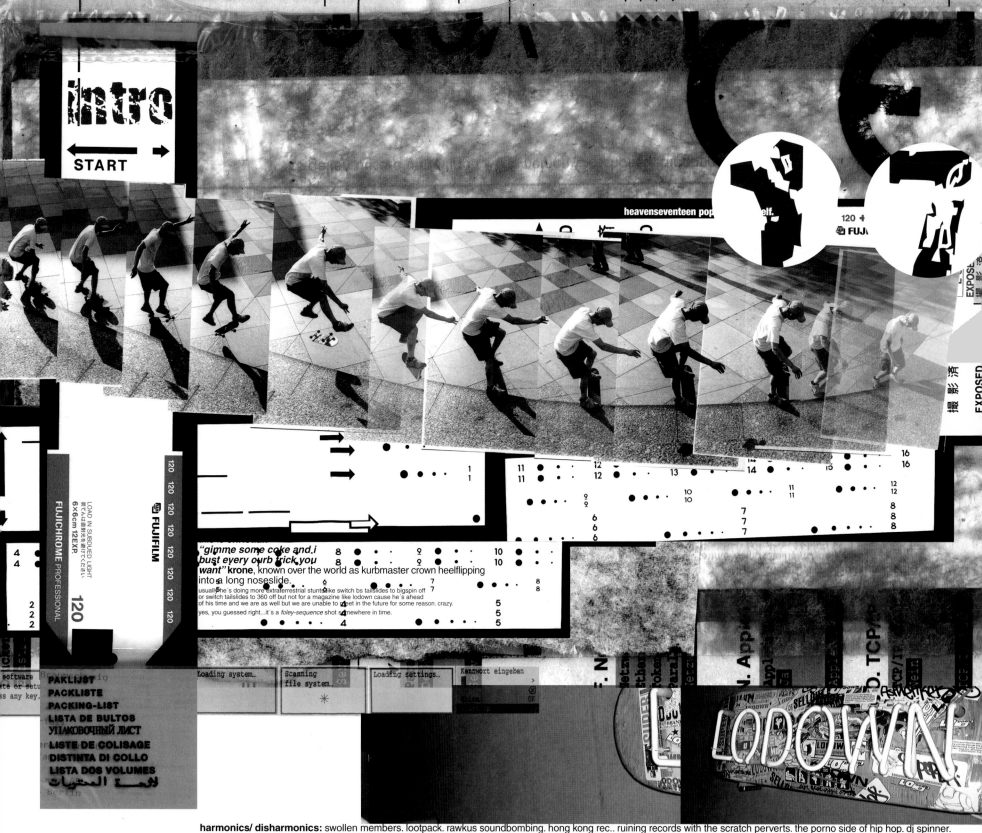

intro

← START →

LOAD IN SUBDUED LIGHT
薄暗い所で光を避けて下さい
6×6cm 12EXP.

FUJIFILM

FUJICHROME PROFESSIONAL

120

"gimme some coke and.i bust every curb trick you want" **krone**, known over the world as kurbmaster crown heelflipping into a long noseslide.

usually he´s doing more extraterrestrial stunts like switch bs tailslides to bigspin off or switch tailslides to 360 off but not for a magazine like lodown cause he´s ahead of his time and we are as well but we are unable to meet in the future for some reason. crazy.

yes, you guessed right...it´s a *foley-sequence* shot somewhere in time.

Loading system... Scanning file system... Loading settings... Kennwort eingeben

LODOWN

harmonics/ disharmonics: swollen members. lootpack. rawkus soundbombing. hong kong rec.. ruining records with the scratch perverts. the porno side of hip hop. dj spinner. sam prekopp. artensemble. **extreme physical ed:** danny supa. wolle nyvelt. hungarian keeper dlx gabor kiraly. milano centrale. lodown zugspitz-kz. vincent gootzen. **general interest questioned:** gordon matter clark. don simpson. shina tsukamoto. gomez bueno. what cannes means to film. star wars meets clerks @ centauri XG74418. jennifer lopez making us crazy. kostas sermites. **photos of people wearing clothes:** eyecandy. nightshift. **more or less thrilling:** thunderbird. helicopter hystery. rock davis rocks again. orel gives you the shit you always wanted. minigolfing. **usus:**laser briefe transmitted by the elektronengehirn. the lack of ideas in the trainer manufacturing business. newsmaker + if you missed the cover check the doc.   this issue features more than 10GB of information. which is more than enough for your intoxicated minds!!!

WHY SECURITY GUARDS PROTECT CONCRETE?
WE KILL STEREOTYPES

one.zero

zeitschrift für populärkultur u. bewegung,

music. sports. entertainment.

LODOWN

2

PLUS **A LOT MORE COLOUR TO YOUR**
VISUAL CONSUMPTION
ALL COMIN' THROUGH IN JULY2000

on the right we got a bs 180 by stephan giret.
below it's christian heitmann hollow man, getting a little bit old school with a big ol' method.
parkinglotsession at friedrichstreet on a rainy day in september 2000
captured by foley

PLAY > CRASH

15

sam harithi plays 16 stairs +
by flachfoto

jan kliewer at the thälmannstatue. east berlin
this is what we call a 'communistblockslide'

PEOPLE OVER THE STAIRS

a compilation of a new generation of daredevils
trying to spill their kneecaps on a spectacular effort

>> the next one is called 'the fearless pritz', dropping a massive double set with ease. you can call 'german flat bomber' too.

by a.d.camera@ostbahnhof berlin

berlin nightshifting, skateboarders faking securityguards
from left to right.
chris heitmann nose- and bluntsliding.
stephan giret from france enjoy's the view at the teletower with a fs noseslide.
lennie burmeister get's underground with an alley oop stalefish at bernd 3000.
till kemner is a grindmachine from berlin, right,
and he knows how to grind impossible spots.

oppositepage:
Don´t get confused with all the colors, the Skateboarder is not a painting,
he is for real and he is really is doing a bs tailslide. by the way this is stephan again.

berlin represent' 00.
foleyfotos

have you seen john travolta dancing in saturday night fever? forget about it and watch sami harithi dancin with this curb! half cab noseslide revert at the philharmonie in 1998.

opposite: 'my life is shooting skateboarders' lifetimemomentum for flachfotographics

lodown

NO TRESPASSING
$ 5.000 FINE OR 10 YEARS IN
PRISON FOR THEFT OF FRUIT

POR EL ROBO DE FRUTA MULTA DE
$ 5.000 O 10 AÑOS DE PRISÍON
NO TRÉSPASEN

its all about property!

co   covershot by tobin yelland in spring 1999,
freezing a moment in julian strangers life somewhere in the early ninties,
when sma was still alive.

PHOTOSURPREME

LODOWN

INTRO

FUCK 'EM ALL

we're eighteen!

...eitmann enjoys the eightees revival, while we're enjoying our adultmentship: to all you crumbsnatchers and bigmoneyshots trying to be like us. fuck you! we rise, you fall, we fall later...

introduction of issue 18.
lodown celebrates the adultstatus

paul machnau has a different way to utilize handrails, but its way faster than the average use.
berlin kunstgewerbe museum, **photo by a.d.**

one night I had this dream. to impress a girl I saw myself sliding down this marble klotz. but then again, one day ed templeton came by and destroyed my dream. boardslide on the most dangerous ledge!
kunstgewerbe museum
photo by alex foley
plus small bitmapped kickflip noseslides by stevee.

the stairs on the left are for walking. robert stoye ollies the cosmos cinema gap.

opposite page:
at enterprise, captain kirk and all his dudes using beams to get down to earth. here we see lennie burmeister using his personal beam, an ollie, to get back to planet earth. potsdamer platz, berlin anno 3000.

christian heitmann with a varial heelflip and a noseslide.
photos by alex foley

gogo on vacation in berlin city, the layout was actually done for a billboard production, but was rejected. hmmm. berlin spring 1999.

ESCAPE

Get The Spirit.

next page:
> **andi traimer.** one epic backside air
    shot at a flumserberg quarterpipesession by andreas töpfer

assist.:
you were looking for that ass? go and find it bear mountain ca. usa
the boy getting the spirit is your loved wolle nyvelt

<< guy kämpfen crosses the kickflipping
dimitry stathis with a nollie heelflip.
please use your red eyes to discover the
blueprint.
**barcelona museum of contemp. art
tortillia jam 2000**

can be found in the National Gallery: the Barcelona Chair. It's a Bauhaus Deluxe item which was manufactured especially for the German pavillion at the 1929 Expo in Barcelona. Mies van der Rohe sampled the essential characteristics of an antique, convertible folding chair and brought them into a new context with chromed steel, leather upholstery and the trademark button pattern.

The chair is pure style and truly impressed the world public in Barcelona. In the same way it now offers in the National Gallery the ideal recreation opportunity in a stylish setting. Apart from being another good skate spot the Bauhaus archive in Berlin gives a good overview of the internal, but also the international styles of the complete Bauhaus staff. Its enormous influence was shown best in the times when most members of the innovative institution had to emigrate to the United States, due to massive harrasment by the Nazis, which helped not only New York with van der Rohe's Seagram building, but also the NY-based designers to profit from a sudden cultural enrichment. A few years later it was a US-American designer couple that were miles ahead of the rest. Charles and Ray Eames worked on a number of production methods, utilising different materials and consequently creating uncountable variations of steel and wooden furniture, which at times you could pile up on top of each other. The best known exponents have just been released in a Girl skateboards range, which again has its origin in the Fresh Jive ad with the Eames Lounge chair, including the miniature chill chair. Charles and Ray Eames had the idea to design the chair when their buddy, director Billy Wilder, didn't feel too comfortable on the usual TV chairs. With the comfort of a baseball glove in mind, the two designers created in 1956 out of single components a sitting chair with Ottoman as leg rest for an excellent TV evening . Wilder then received the cosy piece of furniture for his birthday. Charles and Ray Eames 670 Lounge chair made it into history and a number of furniture catalogues,

nterior Design as continuiation of the rgument with contemporary architecture.

fter skating, you've got to sit down.

he new National Gallery. Built between 1962-1967 by architect Ludwig Mies van der ohe. For more than 10 years Berlin's best known skatespot and in a way the German dition of San Fran's Embacadero, but completely edgy - apart from the curbs. And ome of the 5000 Mark a-piece glas windows, that got destroyed by unidentified flying kateboards. In the course of times a lot of architecture has been added around the ational Gallery, which has been the only building in the middle of nowhere between e Berlin wall and the Landwehr canal, but now is the centre of the whole spot on the real near Potsdamer Platz. It wasn't even supposed to be erected there, because Cuba as also interested in Mies van der Rohe's plans. But luckily enough that fell through, o that Mies van der Rohe - in his own right Germany's most influential architect - elivered enormous foreign aid in terms of skateboarding, still corresponding to the auhaus program `form follows function'.

s Bauhaus director and with his numerous works as architect and furniture designer e has heavily influenced the `International Style' and created the strongest basics for heap building/furniture production, which enabled the average consumer to afford this tyle. Although the Ikea concern is one of the only companies that holds on to these hics. But the slickest sitting opportunity, still holding the Champions place in the style ague after more than 70 years,

thibaud fradin switch crooks in barcelona >>

which offer the timeless classic as a replication for £1700 to £2800. Alternatively, for only £300 you can get the Eames's DCW wooden furniture featured on Koston's board graphic. Both are using diverse materials on their furniture like the RAR Rocking Chair on Colin McCay's deck, which is made of steel, plastic, and wood. Less comfortable but at that time quite progressive, is the plastic bomber DAR with an Eiffel Tower base shown on Howard's plank. All chairs were built after exact ergonomic studies carried out by the Eames couple on leg braces and other orthopaedic device. Tony Ferguson finally chose the most comfortable piece. The Three-Seat-Sofa that Charles Eames designed just before his death in 1979 and that features materials typically used for skateboards. The upholstery consists partly of poly-urethan and the main material is the widely appreciated Plywood, which doesn't make it any cheaper. Also the Barcelona Chair costs somewhere around £700 - £1400, depending on the manufacturer, who may or may not reserve some rights. Weather these are genuine replicas or just cheap copies doesn't matter - as even Mies van der Rohe wouldn't be able to distinguish between them. His credo of wanting to offer his furniture for low prices has, after decades, also ended up on the junk yard.

MUTANTS RELY ON THE DARK
SIDE OF THE MOON.
PLAY THE FIVE TONES.

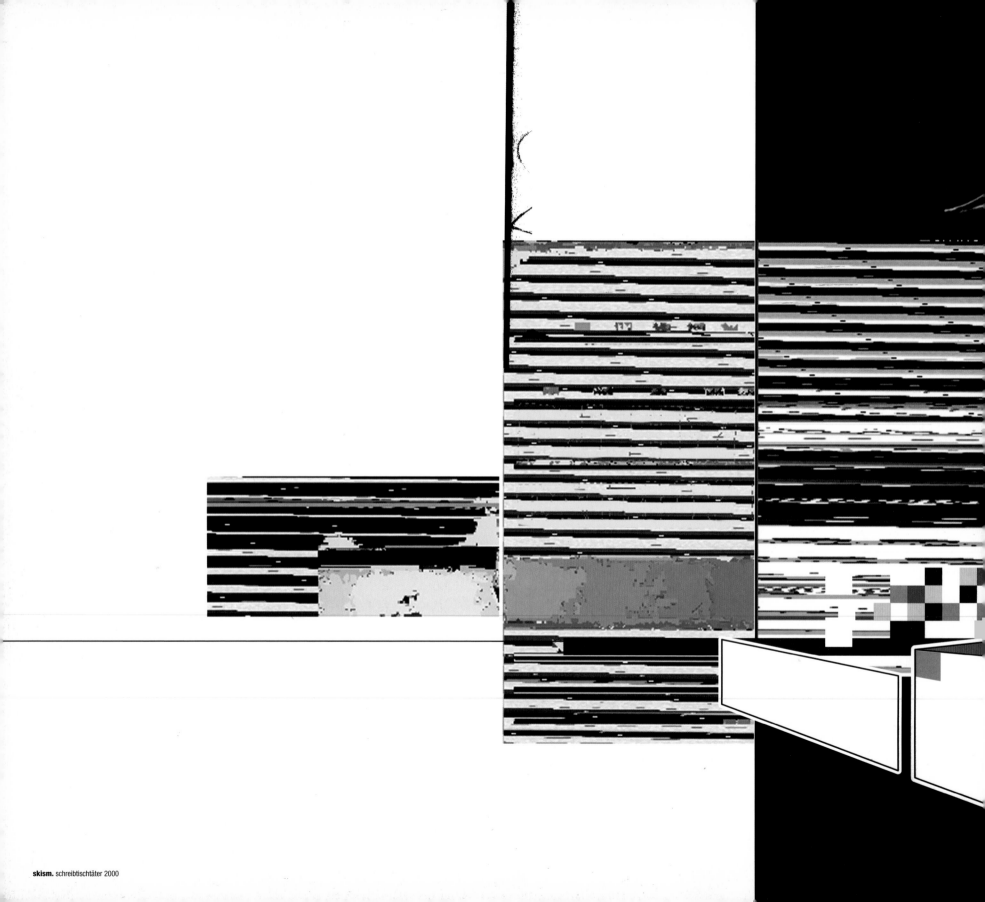

skism. schreibtischtäter 2000

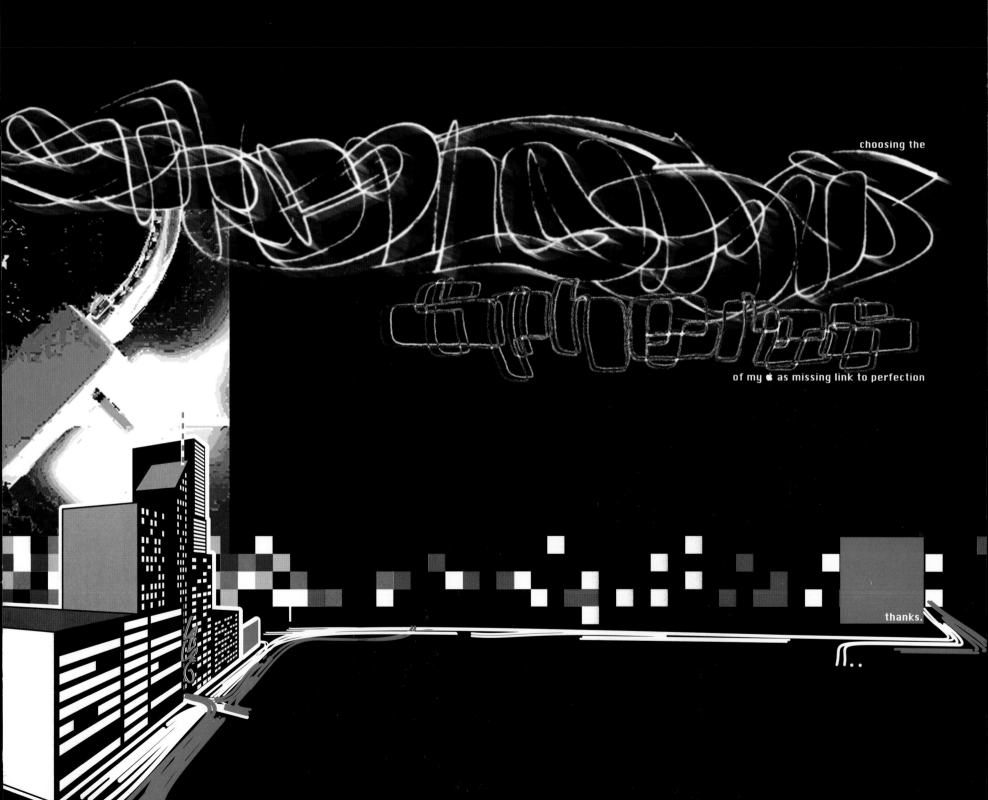

choosing the

of my as missing link to perfection

thanks.
..

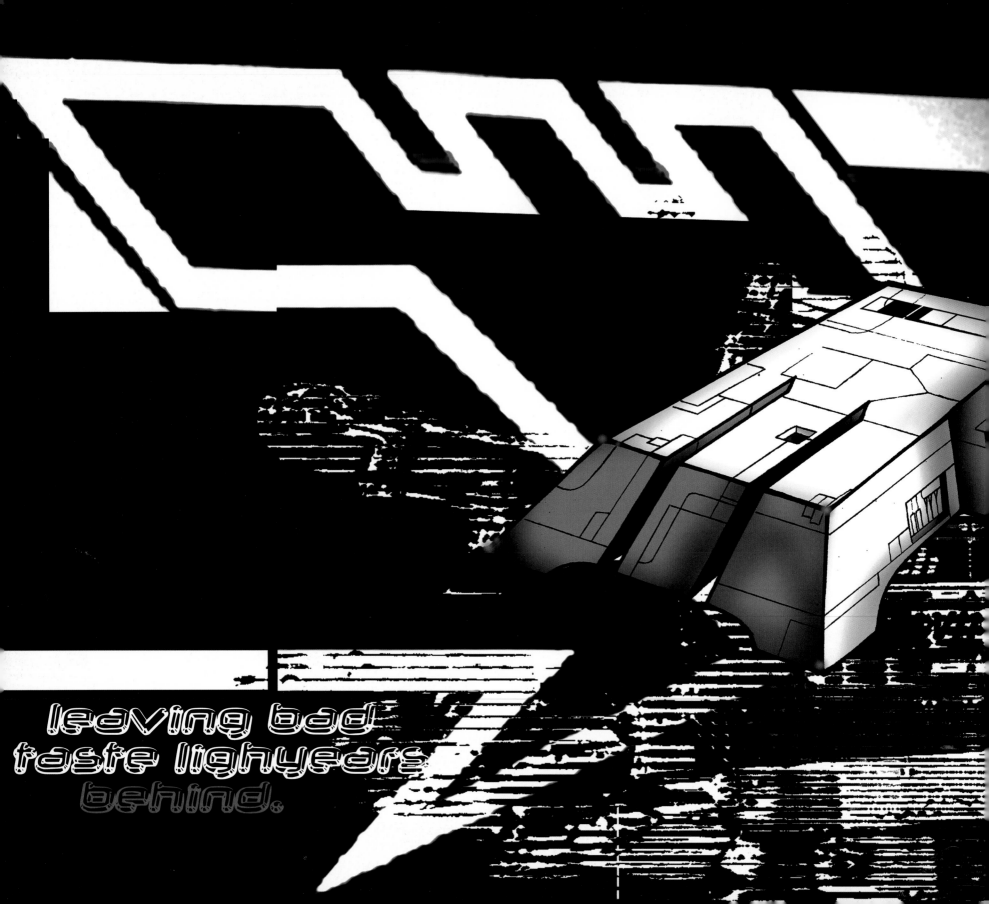

leaving bad
taste lightyears
behind.

Ian Brown
by Stefan Plaetz

Las Vegas, 22 Novembre 1965 . Au cours d'un combat prévu en 15 rounds, Ali met Floyd Patterson K.O. au 12e. Harry Krause, l'arbitre, raconte : "Je lui ai dit : Ça va Floyd tu peux continuer ? Oui il m'a dit . Ça me faisait mal de voir ça, il n'en pouvait plus . Il tenait ses poings comme une petite vieille."

'Ali boma ye!'

EVERLAST

remix.david king 1976

脱勉強

KINSEY - THIS IS SIX PAGES

TAUGHT BELIEVED MISLED MOLDED PURSUED

UNLEAГN

Passion, Practice, Persistence, Patien

RE-ENTER

金勢

Amputate Programmed Thought ENDURE YOUR EXISTANCE

01

BLK/MRKT
CREATIVE VISUAL COMMUN

The idea of using the urban landscape as a canvas remains constant.

キンジィー

®
™
©

FOR THE MORE EXPANDED EXPERIENCE CONNECT TO:
KINSEYVISUAL.COM

romon yang aka ro-starr.**nyc**

Romon is a New York based painter and graphic designer.
As a painter his work weaves a personal vocabulary of iconography
and type into an abstract polymorphic painting style which he calls
'Graphysics'. The diversity of his work can be found on album covers,
t-shirts, magazines as well as in galleries.

robert d. cristofaro aka jest.
born in brooklyn and based in new york

robert is a painter/illustrator/designer who gained recognition for his large, clean, easy to read style. Most of his work was placed in highly visible locations along the major expressways in the New York area. The late eighties throughout the late nineties was the era that the Jest brand was appearing on a consistent level throughout nyc.

jest is an artist that thrives on people viewing his art in the outdoors. his artwork consists of illustration, painting, collage, dollmaking by hand, and typography with the use of rubber stamps and woodblock letters. His newest project is **alife**, a collaborative effort that encompasses design/retail and creative collective based in New York City, which is opened to the public. Founded Oct. 10 1999.

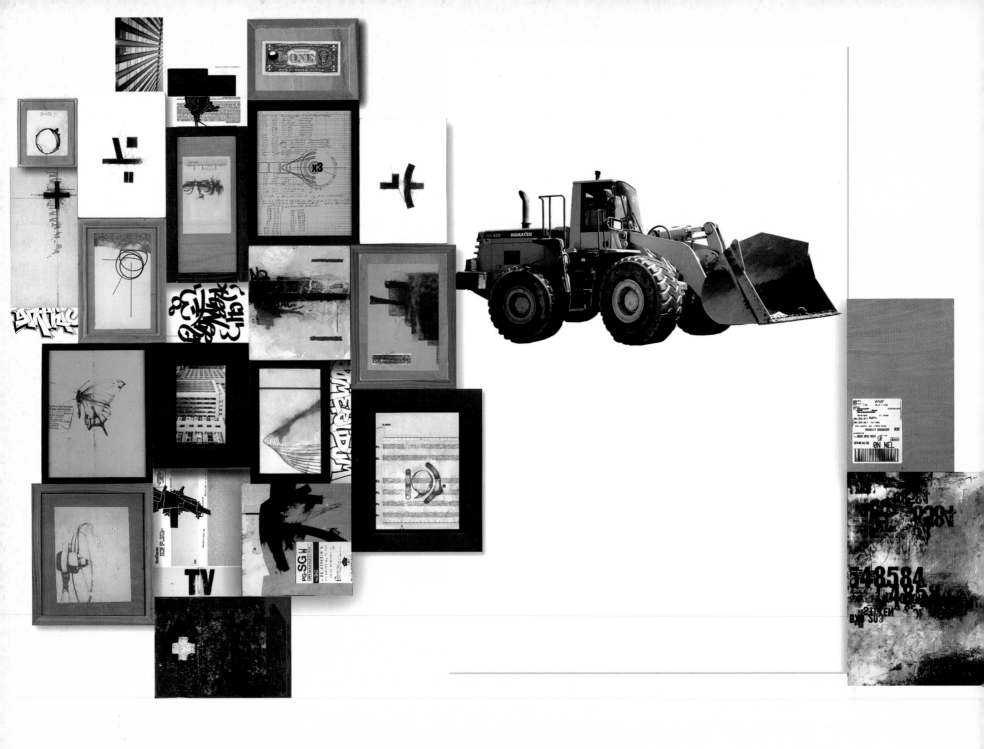

Graphic Havoc avisualagency
brooklyn new york
for more information please pay a visit to www.graphichavoc.com. thank you.

KR is a New York based graffiti writer, photographer, and artist. KR has been writing graffiti and documenting the graffiti lifestyle for close to a decade, as well as working in a number of different mediums including photography, painting, and sculpture.

tony arcabascio aka site
born in 1970 in astoria, queens ny.

looking for means of self-expression in the early 80's, tony becomes involved with bmx freestyling, break dancing, and graffiti.
in the later 80's, tony becomes increasingly attracted by nightlife activities and begins a 6 year career as a dj/club promoter which leads him to produce club flyers, design club interiors, produce artwork for independent record labels and develop a taste for new ways to express his art. soon thereafter he turns his effort to apparel and puts out a line of t-shirts under the name "world ecaep" in 1994. spelling peace backwards, "ecaep" focuses on world chaos and advertises the slogan "do we really want peace?" if everyone in the world really wants peace, why don't we have it?... there are things other than peace, which are "god" to people. things people worship or live for.
a few years later he introduces the next chapter of his world ecaep crusade, now evolved into the "what's your god?" slogan, and proceeds to bomb new york city, and on his travels, with a sticker campaign asking the same question. "the what's your god?" campaign is meant to make you evaluate the importance of your god. what do you worship, adore, praise, lust, and indulge with in your life? what are you addicted to and should it be that important to you? power, sex, money, drugs, attention, fashion, etc... what is god to you?

The Andre the Giant sticker campaign can be explained as an experiment in Phenomenology. Heidegger describes Phenomenology as "the process of letting things manifest themselves." Phenomenology attempts to enable people to see clearly something that is right before their eyes but obscured; things that are so taken for granted that they are muted by abstract observation. The first aim of Phenomenology is to reawaken a sense of wonder about one's environment. The Andre the Giant sticker attempts to stimulate curiousity and bring people to question both the sticker and their relationship with their surroundings. Because people are not used to seeing advertisements or propoganda for which the product or motive is not obvious, frequent and novel encounters with the sticker provoke thought and possible frustration, nevertheless revitalizing the viewer's perception and attention to detail. The sticker has no meaning but exists only to cause people to react, to contemplate and search for meaning in the sticker. Because Andre the Giant has a Posse has no actual meaning, the various reactions and interpretations of those who view it reflect their personality and the nature of their sensibilities. Many people who are familiar with the sticker find the image itself amusing, recognizing it as nonsensical, and are able to derive straightforward visual pleasure without burdening themselves with an explanation. The paranoid or conservative viewer however may be confused by the sticker's persistent presence and condemn it as an underground cult with subversive intentions. Many stickers have been peeled down by people who were annoyed by the sticker which they consider to be an eye sore and an act of petty vandalism, which is ironic considering the number of commercial graphic images that everyone in American society is assaulted with daily. Another phenomenon the sticker has brought to light is society's trendy and conspicuously consumptive nature. For those who have been surrounded by the sticker, its familiarity and cultural resonance is comforting and owning a sticker provides a souvenir or keepsake, a momento. People have often demanded the sticker merely because they have seen it everywhere and possessing a sticker provides a sense of belonging. The Andre sticker seems mostly to be embraced by those who are, or at least want to be, rebellious. Even though these people may not know the meaning of the sticker, they enjoy its slightly disruptive underground quality and wish to contribute to the furthering of its humorous and absurd presence which seems to be anti-establishment/societal convention.

Andre the Giant stickers are both embraced and rejected, the reasoning behind which reflects the psyche of the viewer. Whether the reaction be positive or negative, the sticker's existence is worthy as long as it causes people to consider the details and meanings of their surroundings. In the name of fun and observation, the experiment continues... -Shepard Fairey

obey.

GIANT

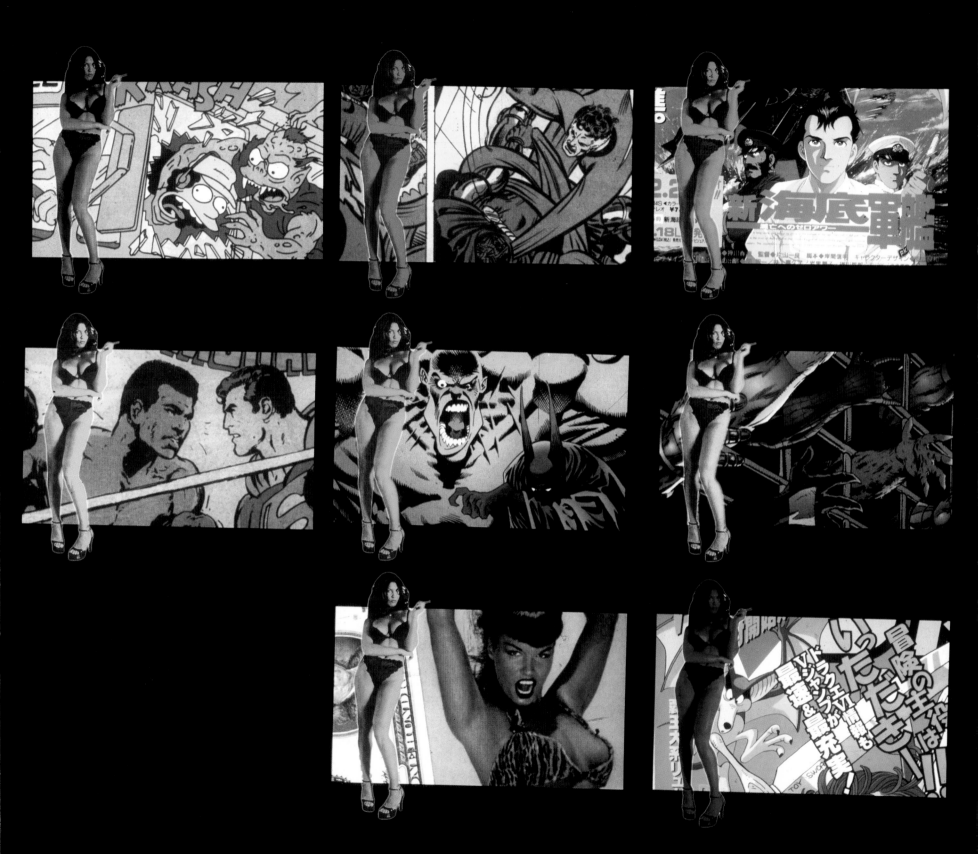

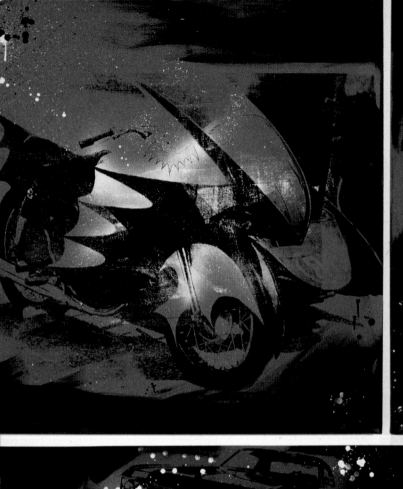
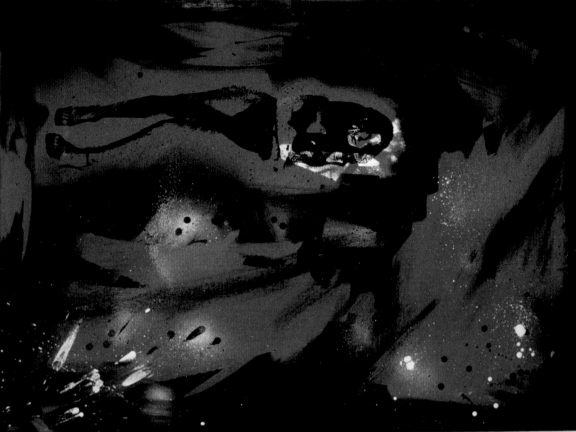
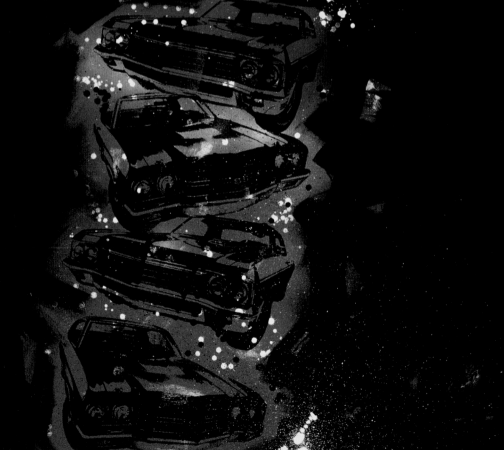

kostas seremetis, paintings out of brooklyn '99-'00

BERLIN STYLE

ERWINDALE RACEWAY   1970-?   PEP

Mark Gonzales

HUNTINGTONPARK HIGH

SELF PORTRAIT

purely promotional
poems by local poet

hy
rite
petry
ny
rite
ything?

lling
o
o I
he
to?

**was hast du
geantwortet?**

I don´t write
poems to be
a poet
I write
them so I can
communicate
that´s a big 10-4
over and out
C.B.
Cisco
this is Big Hammer
do you hear me?

**o.k. noch ein paar persönliche fragen.
was macht der gonz in seiner freizeit?**

LSD that shit´s got me
I quite the brigade
of that uselessness
I got your cash
hidden up my ass.

**was turnt dich
richtig an?**

old ladies
drive crazy
in
brand new
mercedes

**was bedeutet
amerika für dich?**

let´s communicate
isolation
shut off from others
round about
your reputations
thrashed
poor Indians
the white man come
to rape and pillage.

...und californien?

the lonely
road travelled
Nevada
Smith
gunslinger
made his
way to
Hollywood
home of
the freak´s
cardinal.

**kannst du die entstehungsgeschichte der welt,
ihren sinn und inhalt und vor allem den sinn des
lebens kurz für uns zusammenfassen?**

**was hältst du von den jungs von support,
die deine lesung hier in hamburg
organisiert haben?**

left
always
overestimate
your opponent
the good
people
are
always
right
they are right

posing
as a cop
got a badge number
that´s simple
and clean police
protection
AIDS is gonna
stop the stronghold.
my bazooka is
gonna shut you up
the whole police force
at once like a
message from god
mankind is unkind

**glaubst du
an den alten
harry da oben?**

food
stamp
child
wears
an
aggravated
smile
the
church
is
D.M.Z.
alone
oneness
God

**s hast du gemacht, als der erste check monatelang
auf sich warten liess?**

we called
the army
to kill
the termites.

POEMS

VERRY BLUE SKY
FULL BLEED
PHOTOS

SHRINK DOWN
DRAWING OF
BOXERS AND
PUT NEXT TO
MY NAME

WITHOUT NAME

K.HARING
RULES

MARK GONZALES

noch eine letzte message an die kids?

slowly
day
after day
your life
will start
to have less
meaning.

suggests very blue sky

TEXAS RADIEO

IU LOST MY PATIENCE WITH THESE LOW DOWN TYPES. M. GONZALES

hi mark, wie geht´s?

not to sound demented or anything but I like to shoot the fucker in the armpit. just stick the gun to his armpit like as if it was deodorant and POW!

o.k., aber wir haben mal ein paar fragen zu dir!

do as I say and no one gets hurt

wie war das damals, mit natas, als ihr die ersten und einzigen wart, die schon street-ollies konnten und handrails slideten, als alle anderen noch fest mit dem boden verankert waren. viele hielten das damals für trickaufnahmen. man sagte ihr habt mit spiegeln gearbeitet?

pin the fucker down I wanna blow off his ankles loud mouth skateboarder.

wart ihr euch der tatsache bewusst, dass ihr eine neue ära im skateboarding eingeläutet habt?

we are the dreamers of the dreams

gibt es eine witzige story von den dreharbeiten?

he planted a bomb at the bank. it will blow at 12:00 noon. set the fire alarm so no one gets hurt.I got to the bank at fifteen to 12:00 to set off the fire alarm but the bank was demolished. I think they wanted to kill me.

hast du mal überlegt, dass du stinkreich sein könntest, wenn du alle deine tricks zum patent gemeldet hättest? ich denke da nur an kickflips, ollie grabs, handrail grinds, fakie kickflips, fs 180 ollies to bw nosegrinds, overturned 180´s to bw grinds (fs & bs), fs varials, fs boardslides, darkslides, darkslides on handrails, late shovits, bw manuals, kink rails, stalefishs, huge stalefishs, huge and stylish stalefishs, streetplants, plus the EMB gonz-gap, the fat fs tweak down the four @ wallenberg, the monster ramp gap fs ollie @ hawaii, eggplants in absolut jeder rampe...

selfish people fill their selfish needs

wer will dir denn schlechtes... ?

quiet. that´s the uncle that was in vietnam

...und, was hat er gantwortet?

if I was half as intelligent as you I´d find better ways to spend my time

aber du hättest damit richtig asche machen können!

rich people´s drama I haven´t got time

du bist wohl der meistrespektierteste skateboarder der welt. jeder andere pro kann durch ein paar falsche tricks, ein falsches wort, durch zu enge hosen, der falschen frisur oder durch skaten am falschen spot sein jahrelang ge-pflegtes image ruinieren. wie fühlt man sich als unfehlbare skatelegende?

the light that is on the other end is a real mind bender connected and inseparable from infinity it is divinity

was bedeutete dir blind?

destructive little fucker react the son of a bitch has gone passive on me

das blind video »video days« ist noch immer für viele der blueprint des modernen skatevideos...

the theater is empty that´s what the movie suggests to its audience

wie macht man solch ein zeitloses und somit immer noch modernes video?

cocain speed acid romantic druggies get high just like in Drugstore Cowboy actual film footage of PCP users freaking out to some that may not be as glamorous how about driving into a wall I thought it was a freeway on-ramp.

blind war mit mariano, johnson, richter, lee und dir eines der fettesten teams überhaupt. warum habt ihr die company verlassen? was hast du steve rocco gesagt als du gingst?

ultimate rejection: take your money and fuck off.

I was writing about vomit. then I got sad. after a few years I kept writing about more vomit. I felt better then I started writing on walls. stuff like »fuck Karl Marx« stupid communist

danach war´s erst mal etwas ruhiger und man sagt, du warst eine zeit lang in frankreich. was hast du gemacht?

warst du in frankreich oft skaten?

I shotgunned that old cannon. the steel was smooth as ever like nothing has happened. »All father are know-it-alls« but not my dad.

jetzt bist du wieder in den staaten und skatest hart wie immer. spürst du nicht langsam das alter in deinen knochen?

dein alter teamkollege jason lee ist inzwischen schauspieler und konnte schon in mehreren filmen sein können zeigen. du kämpfst in harmony corine´s »gummo« mit einem stuhl. könnte die schauspielerei eine weitere profession für die zukunft sein?

I tried to give a new meaning to the word definition did I ask if the poem lacked in structure?

klar, verständlich...

I grant you understanding as of now you will be known as the conqueror of e rrr oR

the average person is subjected to so much abuse. take the basic sales pitch for example.

nö, ist aber nicht so schlimm.

man könnte also auch sagen, dass...?

you´re not making sense like as if I´m supposed to

schon seit einigen jahren schreibst du kurzgeschichten für´s thrasher mag. war das deine idee?

I´m gonna call this mine. a plastic gun filled with wine I´m a drunk with a busy mind that passes time by writing poems who needs a squirt plum wine it won´t hurt.

I LIKE SKATEBOARDING BUT I HATE THE PRESHER OF HAUEING TO PROOFE MYSELF @ TO ME I SKATE AS A FORM OF EXPRESHION. DO NEW COMPLEX TRICKS. JUST PUSH AND GO WITH OUT OLLING

fiGht hiGht

steve BERRa - clocks - los angeles, ca
Nineteen 98 →

mike connolly → N.Y.C. - t-Messian tech. 1997

BRIAN Summer → orbital ollie
Hong kong airport →
Nineteen 98

Jonny BATLey - fez, North AFRica, Maroc
Contimplation 1997 t. Mc e

"This is a note about my work which comes in many mediums. The ones that have scratched their way to the surface are pigments (paint) applied to various surfaces, film in its still and moving states, scribble (writing) and sometimes the combination of all of these elements to make pies for the eyes. I try to live my life in a creative movement, adapting this to whatever format, making stuff, food, music, sculpture, love, and riding on water and land. It's my goal to do everything from a heart level. I'm not totally there by any means, but I'm trying. Making stuff help me get out the crap that needs to be freed. So it's the process that helps to balance everything, not necessarily the product. I guess I'm not trying to tell you, the specific reader, I'm just trying to keep my heart good, and stuff-making is my path."

thomas campbell likes to travel and lives now in santa cruz california, usa

thomas campbell
black and white studio installation
photographs by cyntia connoly

--------------47F34ADDAFFE6B5DC11E3EDE
Content-Type: image/ORG; x-mac-type="4A504547"; x-mac-creator="0919234599";
 name="ARKITIPISSUE.5"
Content-Transfer-Encoding: base05
Content-Description: Unknown Document
Content-Disposition: OFFline;
 filename="ARKITIPISSUE.5"

/9j/4AAQSkZJRgABAgEASABIAAD/7QIIUGhvdG9zaG9wIDMuMAA4QkINA+kAAAAAAHgAKAAA
AEgASAAAAAAC5wJS//f/9wMPAIsgAgUoA/wAAAAAAWgBaAAAAAAOgwuaAXQAMguaSKgASwAB
AQEAAAABJw8AAQABAAAAAAAAAAAAAAAAAAAAAAAAAAAAAAAQBkAwAAAAAAAAAACAxBAgiAAIA
AAAADUGaiA4QkINA+0AAAAABAASAAAAAEAAQBIAAAAAQABOEJJTQNAAAAAAAEAAAAeDhC
SU0D8wAAAAAACAAAAAAAAAAOEJJTQQKAAAAAAABAAA4QkINJxAAAAAAAoAAQAAAAAAAAC
OEJJTQP1AAAAABIAC9mZgABAG xmZgAGAAAAAAABAC9mZgABAKGZmgAGAAAAAABADIAAAAB
AFoAAAGAAAAAAABADUAAAABAC8AAAGAAAAAAABOEJJTQP4AAAAABwAAD///////////////
//////////////A+gAAAA//////////////////////////////wPoAAAAP//////////
//////////////8D6AAAAD//////////////////////////////A+gAADhCSU08ECAAA
AAAAEAAAAEAAAAJAAAACQAAAAA4QkINBBQAAAAAAAAQOEJJTQQAAAAAAAAAHAAUBQAQAB
AQD//4gxYSUNDX1BST0ZJTEUAAQEAAAxITGlubQIQAABtbnRyUkdCIFhZWiAHzgACAAkABGAx
AABhY3NwTVNGVAAAAABJRUMgc1JHQgAAAAAAI   DTLUhQICAAAAA
AAAAAAAAAAAAAAAAAAAAAAAAAAAAAAAAAAAAAAAAI   iiiiiiiiiiiiiiiiiiiLFjcHJ0AAAABUAAA
ADNkZXNjAAAAAGx3AAAABAhHR0AAAB8AAAABRia. IACBAAAABRyUFIaAAACGAAAABRnWFIa
AAACLAAAABRiWFIaAAAACQAAABRkbW5k5kAAACUI IBkbWRkAAACxAAAAIh2dWUkAAADTAAA
AIZ2aWW3AAAD1AAAACRsdW1pAAAD+AAAABRtZI   iAEDAAAACR0ZUMNoAAAEMAAAAAxYUFJD
AAAEPAAAACAuUFJDAAAEPAAAACAxiUFJDAAAEP| 07Vk9000000ENvcHlyaWdodCRoYykg
MTk5OCBIZXdsZXR0LXBXR0lUBhY2thcU9Q29tcGFuef   lASc1JHQiBJRUM2MTk2Ni006
Ni0yLjEAAAAP   iiiiiiiiiiiQiiiiiiiiiiiiAAAAAAHTTP://
AAAAAAAAAAE   AAAAAAAAAAAAAAWFIaIAAAAAAAAAF   EAAAABFsxY'WWW
AAAAAAAAAE   AAAAAAABvogAAAOPUAAAOQWFIaIP   AAAGKZ-ARKITIP
GNpYWUogA   2z2R1c2MAAAAAAAAFKiIFQyBodH   8vd3d3Lm11YCOM
aAAAAAAAE   #0i8vd3d3LmllYy5jaAAAAAAAAAA   AAAAAAAAAAAAAAA
AAAAAAAAAE   AAAAAABkZXNjAAAAAAAAAAC5JRU   E5NjYtMi4xIERI
2hF1bHQlk   FIZSAtIHNSAAAAAAAAAAAAAAAA   MgNjE5NjYtMi4x
ER1ZmF   iDzcGFjZ29t   AAAAAAAAAAAAAAA
GUzYwU   H1IFZpZXdI   1uItIFQzYxOTY2LTIiu
1AAAAA   ZSBWaWV   BpbiBJRUM2MTk2Ni0y
IGAAAA   AAABOk/gAUXy4AEM8UAAPtzAAE
UgBQF   AAAAAAAAAAAAAAAAAAAAAA
WUIQgY   QAAAAABQAKRAA8AFAARZAB4AIwAo
ogBiAA   HCBAIYAiwCQAJUAmgCfAKQAqQCu
EC   2wENARMBGQEfASUBKwEyATgBPgFF
hp   HJAdEB2QHhAekB8gH6AgMCDAIU
SR   LBAssC1QLgAusC9QMAAAwsDFgMh
tL   5BAYEEwQgBC0EOwRIBFUEYwRx
h6   iBYYFIgHmBbUFxQXUBeUF9gYG
k   B08HYQd0B4YHmQesB78H0gfI
th   PCHQJeQmPCaQJugnPCeUJ+woR
SR   PC8gL4Qv5DBIMKgxDDFwMdQyO
A   ZuN80mw62Dt107g8JDyUPQQ9e
                                                                         EYwRqhHJEegSBxxImEkUS2BKE
hp   MFPAUEhU8FVYUeBWBFb0U4BYD
SR   GK8Y1Rj6GSAZRRIrGZEZtxnd
hb   Iwc9R0eHUcdcB2ZHcMd7B4W
ch6   98THz4fa   fb   CVi   UghdSGhIc4h+yInIIUigiKv
                                                                         cmVyaHJrcm6CcYJ0kneier
                                                                         2k2krnSuRLAUsOSxuLKIs1y0M
uFi5MLoIuty   bMRIxSjGCMbox8jIqMmMymzLU

Question: "Are they here to save us from ourselves?"

It was inevitable perhaps that someone would propound the theory that the UFO's are angelic, at least by intent, coming here on a mission of mercy to the world. That's a mighty comforting hypothesis—and a mighty thin one.

The first mass sighting of the saucers did not occur until two years after we exploded our first atomic bomb. In fact, we had exploded several of them before Ken Arnold spotted his weird aerial contemporaries. There has been nothing to indicate that the UFO's have been unusually interested in the atomic installations, tests or storage points. There has been nothing to indicate that to the Unknowns who direct the saucers we are more than a passing curiosity, merely interesting creatures crawling around on one of the minor bodies of a boundless universe, inspection and examination.

SCOTT ANDREW SNYDER
ASSORTED PHOTOGRAPHY
FOR
ARKITIP.

scott snyder, los angeles, usa

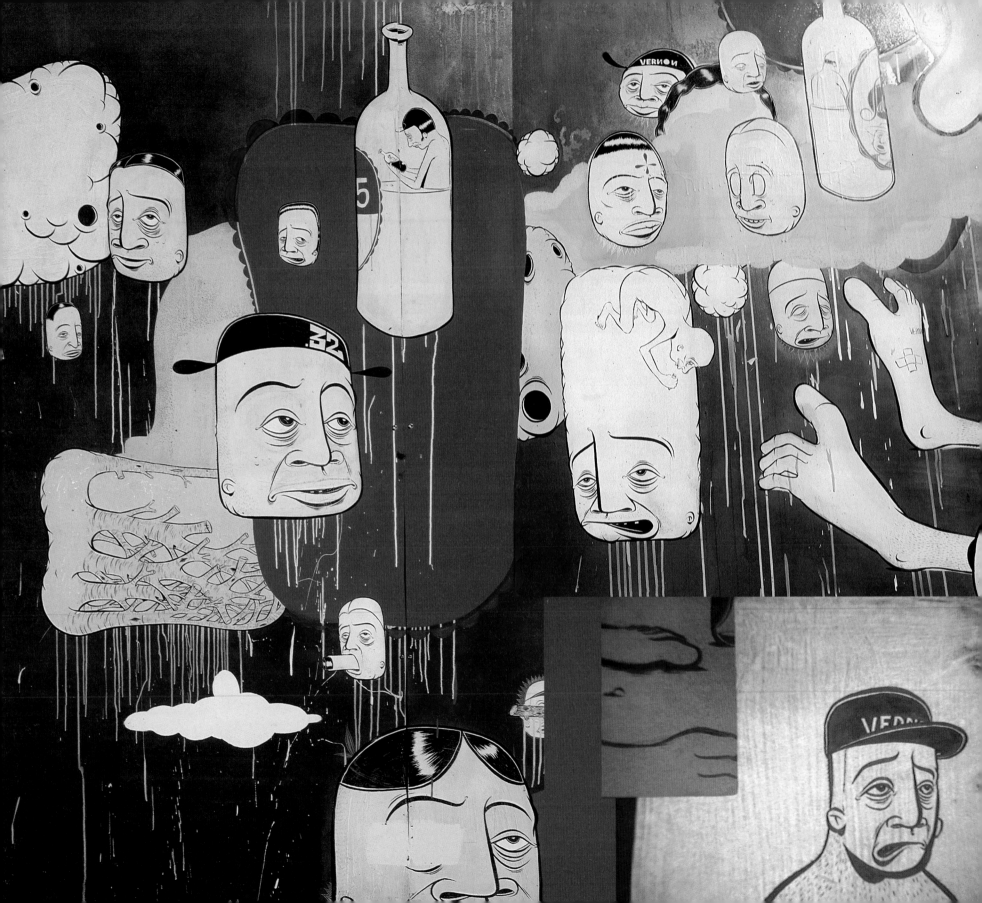

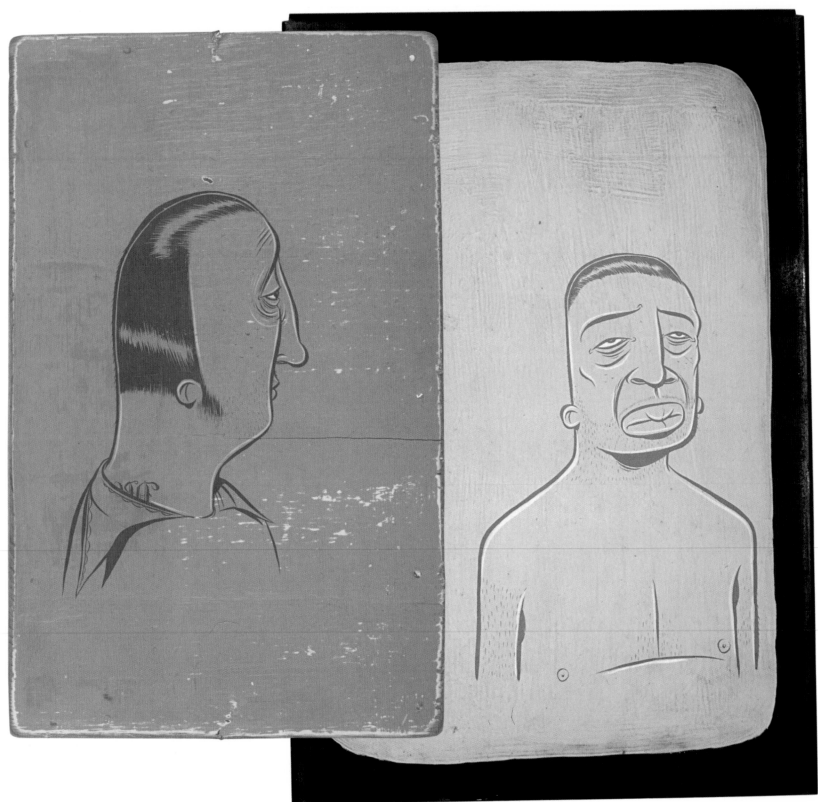

twist aka barry mc gee born 1966 in san francisco.

studiotime in 1997, shot by thomas campbell

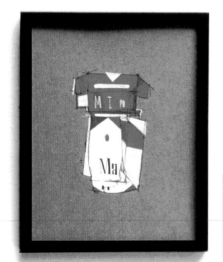

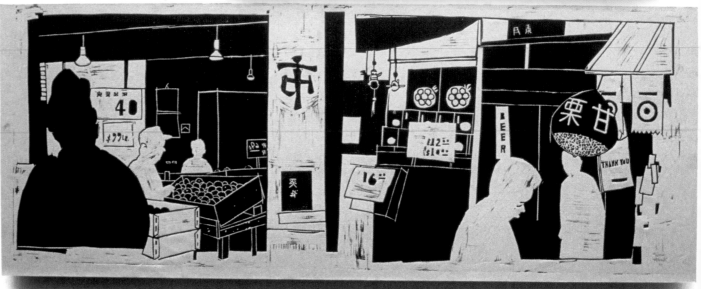

*headphones
required*

"my recent work consists of paintings and prints wich take their inspiration from observations of the world around me. I am fascinated with cities and the complexity of the urban landscape, people, color, signage, graffiti, grime, and deterioration. I try to have a different perspective of my environment and extract beauty from mundane and familiar surroundings that people would normally overlook. as I progress I find that the subject matter that I choose is driven by a sense of abstraction. I find myself simplifying forms and colors, breaking down images, removing certain elements while emphasizing others. much of my work is very small, I like the intimate feeling that small pieces have, engaging the viewer, drawing them in to look more closely, to become absorbed in the work. I like to show various pieces in small clusters that work together to create a greater feeling than a single piece would have by itself." **evan hecox**

THROTTLE YOUR THROAT
AND
BURN KEROSENE
THE ILLFAVORED LODOWNMAG TURNS
TWENTYONE

samples of my work **1997 to 2000** >> **next sixteen pages.**

l.a. drive by die aushöhlung der institutionen, long beach, ca usa

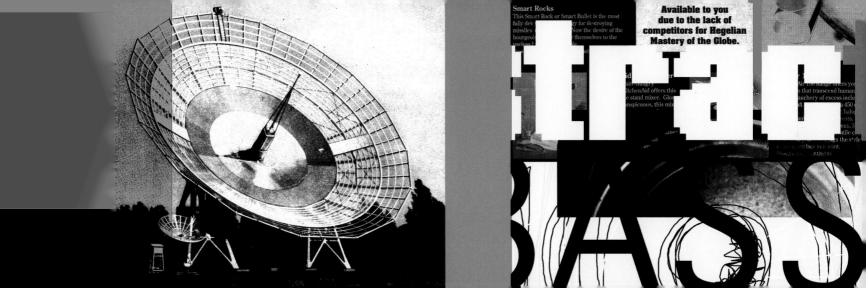

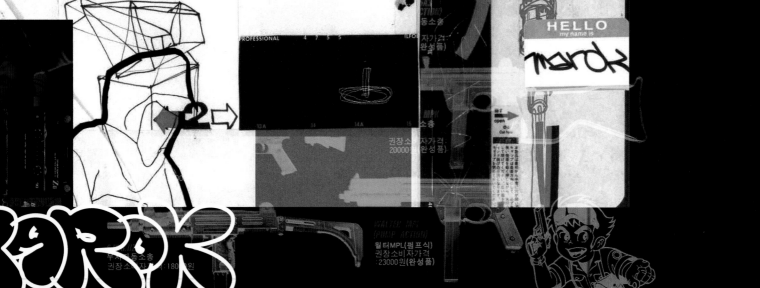

transforming rapcity relics into wooden frames **part II**

'marok over great american money' **nyc 2000**

'neon domination',1998
opposite page:
a lodown blackbox installation for hongkong,2000

all studiophotographs by alexander foley

ANTHONY'S HUGE SHIFTY & BS'S BY REDA
THE NEW MIX TAPE 2 VIDEO IA PRODUCTION
CHECK THE WEB SITE FOR MORE DETAILS
WWW.ZOOYORK.COM
BIG UPS TO KING MEAT - ROCKIN' IT

Synott RD 6700

𝔄NTHONY 𝔏ORREA

Fs Backside Shifty

PRIME CUT: 𝒁oo 𝔜ork

Fs 2 Backside Tailslide

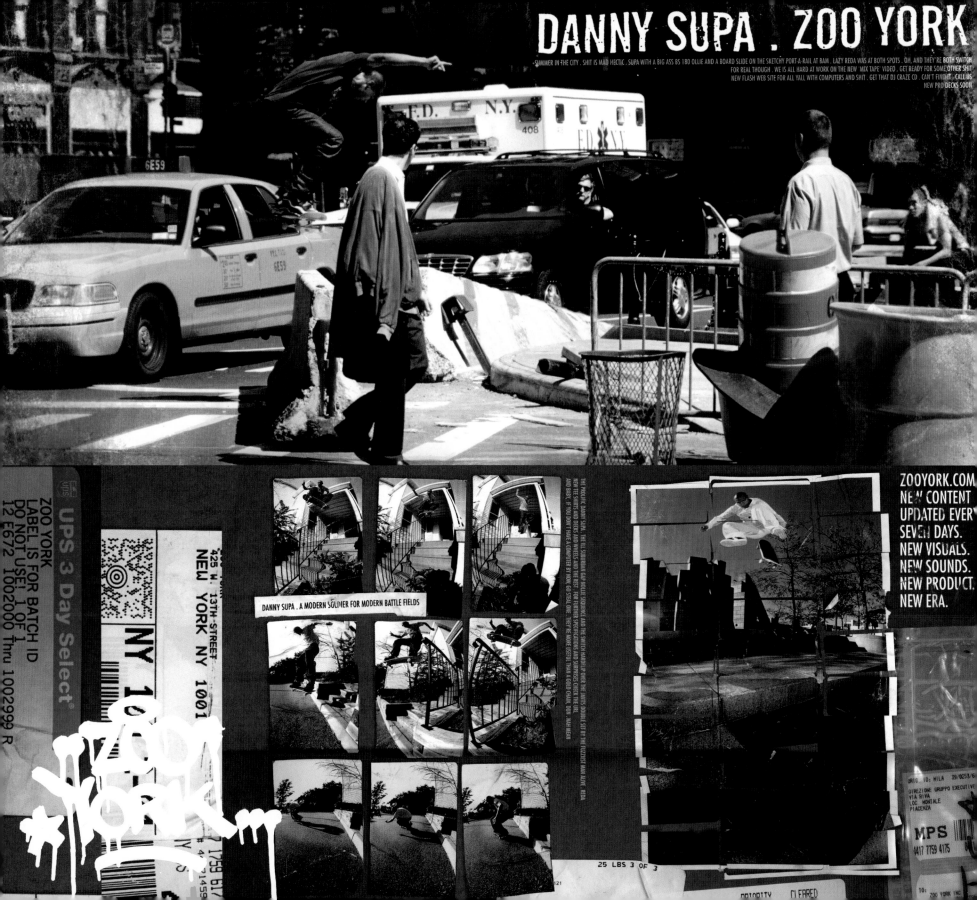

DANNY SUPA . ZOO YORK

· SUMMER IN THE CITY . SHIT IS MAD HECTIC . SUPA WITH A BIG ASS BS 180 OLLIE AND A BOARD SLIDE ON THE SKETCHY PORT-A-RAIL AT BAM . LAZY REDA WAS AT BOTH SPOTS . OH, AND THEY'RE BOTH SWITCH
FOR REAL THOUGH . WE IS ALL HARD AT WORK ON THE NEW 'MIX TAPE' VIDEO . GET READY FOR SOME OTHER SHIT
NEW FLASH WEB SITE FOR ALL YALL WITH COMPUTERS AND SHIT . GET THAT DJ CRAZE CD . CAN'T FIND IT . CALL US
NEW PRO DECKS SOON

ZOOYORK.COM
NEW CONTENT
UPDATED EVERY
SEVEN DAYS.
NEW VISUALS.
NEW SOUNDS.
NEW PRODUCT.
NEW ERA.

DANNY SUPA . A MODERN SOLDIER FOR MODERN BATTLE FIELDS

THE PROLIFIC DANNY SUPA . THE ILL SUBURBAN GAP MOLLIE SEQUENCE AND THE SWITCH HARDFLIP OVER THE ANYTS DOUBLE SET BY THE FUZZIEST MAN ALIVE : REDA
NEW TEE SHIRTS AND DECKS, AND WHEELS AND THE REST . FOR FURTHER SPECIFICATIONS AND SURPRISES CHECK THE URL
AND BABY , IF YOU DON'T HAVE A COMPUTER BY NOW GO STEAL ONE . THEY'RE MORE USEFUL THAN A GOLD CHAIN . DUH . NAH MEAN

THIS AD IS DEDICATED WITH ALL OUR LOVE AND RESPECT TO OUR BROTHER, VICTIM CHARLES PIERCE. JUSTIN WAS A TRUE FRIEND TO ALL OF US HERE AT ZOO YORK AND WAS ONE OF THE TRUE ORIGINAL HOMIES OF OUR CLUB. HE WILL BE MISSED BY US ALL BUT HE WILL NEVER BE FORGOTTEN AT ZOO YORK AS TODAY. JUSTIN HELPED IN THE EVOLUTION OF WHO WE WERE NOTHING. EVERYONE HERE AT ZOO ALL THAT ZOO YORK IS TODAY. JUSTIN HELPED IN THE EVOLUTION OF WHO WE WERE NOTHING. EVERYONE HERE AT ZOO ANYONE WHO EVER RODE FOR US, EVERYONE THROUGHOUT ZOO'S ILLUSTRIOUS HISTORY THAT WAS FORTUNATE ENOUGH TO KNOW JUSTIN. FEELS THE MOST SINCERE LOSS . ALL OF OUR HEARTS GO OUT TO YOU AND YOUR FAMILY OUR THOUGHTS WILL BE WITH YOU FOREVER. REST IN PEACE AND LIVE ETERNALLY IN OUR HEARTS. PEACE

. SAME PHOTOG . GIO REDA . NO MORE FUCKING AROUND .   NEVER UNDERESTIMATE THE ZOO . NEVER

BURTON SMITH ON THE HALF CAB / FAKIE OLLIE / SWITCH BACKSIDE 180 RAIL DUTIES . SAME SESSION

STAINLESS STEEL

Todd Jordan

WWW.
Zoo
York
.COM

FUTURA LABORATORIES
DRAGON EXPERIMENT: ANIMAL BEHAVIOR

FL

Has llegado a esta página por resultado de un error.

Futura A1 naar de hoofdklasse !

CHASSIS: akselafstand 1010 - 1270 mm. med max 80 Ø b

MOTOR: KOMET K25 - DINO - 543/544/545/546/547/548

Enhver form for modifikation på anledning på nogen af mot

KOMET K25 's homologation nr. efter DASU d

Karburator: Tillotson HL 334/A/C 325

Lydpotte: 0

Kobling: Iame Parilla - an - FMK 19/95/05/95 homologe

Indsugningsdæmper: K homologeret.

DINO: homologation og efter DASU datablad

Karburator: Tillotson 348

Lydpotte: 19/95/05/95 og 14 ADAG homologationsp

Kobling: homologationspapirer.

Indsugningsdæmper: K homologeret.

ROTAX 125 MAX.: efter DASU datablade.

Karburator: standard iflg. DASU datablade.

Lydpotte: standard iflg. DASU datablade.

Kobling: standard iflg. DASU datablade.

Indsugningsdæmper: Standard original dæmper med filter.

Karrosseri: efter 64.020

Dæk: se punkt 64.007

Alder: fra 16 år.

Vægt: minimum 155 kg

Numre: sorte tal på gul plade

Mesterskab: intet.

Støjgrænse: 79 db(A) - 77 db(A) i år 2000

Startmetode: stående

Tænding: der må anvendes tændingsafbrydere.

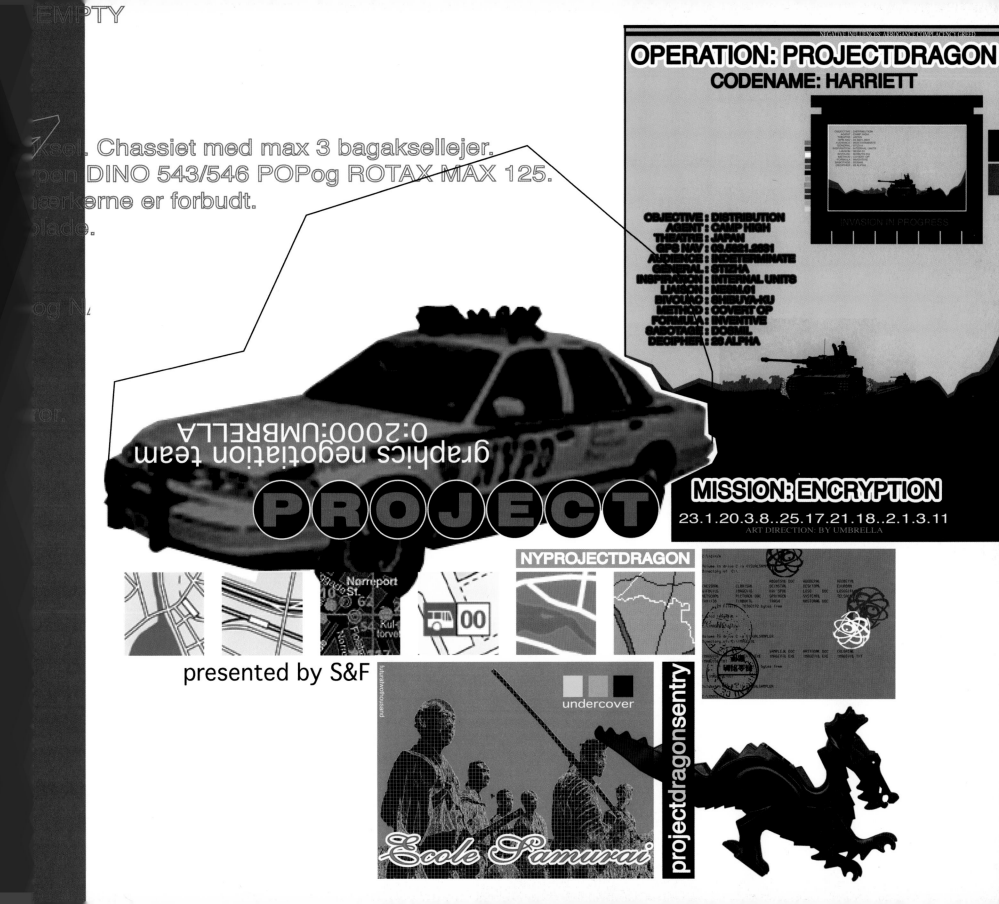

RECON.TRIANGLE

enhance rotoscan

3CONPARK
OPTICAL SCHEMATIC

SPEC OPS
SAN FRANCISCO
RECON

```html
<html>
<head>
<center><TITLE>my lips are moving but you're not hearing me</TITLE>
<BODY BGCOLOR="#000000" TEXT="#FFFFFF>
<BR>
<center><FONT SIZE=8 COLOR=#222222>thoughts on the process of moving beyond
the stereotypes of yesteryear</A></center>
<BR>
<center><FONT SIZE=8 COLOR=#FFFFFF>
what do i know about anything beyond my own personal experiences and observations???
as a writer from "back in the day", i can only be optimistic regarding the future of our culture.
less concerned am i to see my own name >in lights< than i am to see
others brought from the shadows and into the mix.</A></center>
<BR>
<center><FONT SIZE=8 COLOR=#FFFFFF>
these other lesser known individuals,
who have made thankless contributions to a movement spanning some thirty years.
nameless, style-less, faceless: famous, infamous, pioneering:
these "kids>now<men>women" have inspired generations.
locally it all grows from reputation, talent and fame. respect comes from those who deserve it.
the childlike game of >show and tell<</A></center>
<BR>
<center><FONT SIZE=8 COLOR=#FFFFFF>
the new get their education from the old and they become the influence of tomorrow.
the cycle is completed when student will become teacher.
is position of education of responsibility.</A></center>
<BR>
<center><FONT SIZE=8 COLOR=#FFFFFF>
who will accept the challenge to take this youth into the future?
can this change and social phenomenon occur on its own terms?
will others ever understand their legacy to the community?
is "the message" only personal?
aren't we communicating with the people around us?
eventually you must contribute to the society that has created you.
and what are the consequences of the things that cannot be controlled?</A></center>
<BR>
<center><FONT SIZE=8 COLOR=#future>INDETERMINATE</A></center>
<BR>
<center><FONT SIZE=8 COLOR=#FFFFFF>over the past five years i have presented
my images/language/design/signature to the global community via the world wide web.
a quantum leap from the humble beginnings of your intrepid author.
there is no comparison to the level of exposure available in this new medium.
what once was a wild, in a subway station on a deserted
platform is now a monitor in a young girl>boy's bedroom.
there i am, in Bosnia, Brasil, Berlin and Bangkok.</A></center>
<BR>
<center><FONT SIZE=8 COLOR=#FFFFFF>in addition to my personal propaganda procedure:
am giving respect and love to a tradition of imagined excellence.
those who were there know, those who were not, will always wonder.
this is relative to where you are; and what is happening around you,
but it all can be changed. i am living proof.</A></center>
<BR>
<center><FONT SIZE=8 COLOR=#222222>because this is my story, and i own it.</A></center>
<BR>
<center><P><FONT SIZE=8 COLOR=#future>
<A HREF="currently.htm" onMouseOver="window.status='SALMA';return true'>
salma</A></center>
<BR>
<center><IMG SRC="timefuk.gif"></center>
<BR>
<BR>
<center><P><FONT SIZE=11 COLOR=#6gg33>
<A HREF="my.htm" onMouseOver="window.status='dangerous';return true'>
almost looks like i shot myself with the LOMO</A></FONT></center>
<BR>
<BR>
<BR>
</body>
</html>
```

LONDON
MO WAX

PARIS
AGNES B

ROSA
PROJECTDRAGON

BERLIN
LODOWN

MODENA
CUBE

SUPREME
RECON
PROJECTDRAGON
UMBRELLA
NEW YORK
SUBWARE
FUTURALABORATORIES
KOSTASYSTEMS
SSUR
STUSSY

TOKYO

TOKION
HECTIC
UNDERCOVER
GENOTYPE
WTAPS
RECON
BATHING APE
BOUNTY HUNTER
NEIGHBORHOOD
ONE GRAM

FUKUOKA
FUTURALABORATORIES

```html
<html>
<head>
<center><TITLE>my lips are moving but you're not hearing me</TITLE>
<BODY BGCOLOR="#OOOOOO"  TEXT="#FFFFFF">
<BR>
<center><FONT SIZE=8 COLOR=#222222>thoughts on the process of moving beyond
the stereotypes of yesteryear</A></center>
<BR>
<center><FONT SIZE=6 COLOR=#FFFFFF>
what do I know about: anything beyond my own personal experiences and observations???
as a writer from "back in the day" I can only be optimistic regarding the future of our culture.
less concerned am I to see my own name >in lights< than I am to see
others brought from the shadows and into the mix.</A></center>
<BR>
<center><FONT SIZE=6 COLOR=#FFFFFF>
these other lesser known individuals,
who have made thankless contributions to a movement spanning some thirty years.
nameless, styleless, faceless: famous, infamous, pioneering:
these "kids/now: men/women" have inspired generations.
locally it all grows from reputation, talent and fame. respect comes from those who deserve i
the childlike game of >show and tell<</A></center>
<BR>
<center><FONT SIZE=6 COLOR=#FFFFFF>
the new get their education from the old and they become the influence of tomorrow.
the cycle is completed when student will become teacher.
a position of education of responsibility.</A></center>
<BR>
<center><FONT SIZE=6 COLOR=#FFFFFF>
who will accept the challenge to take this youth into the future?
can this change and social phenomenon occur on its own terms?
will writers ever understand their legacy to the community?
is "the message" only personal?
aren't we communicating with the peoples around us?
eventually you must contribute to the society that has created you.
and what are the consequences of the things that cannot be controlled?</A></center>
<BR>
<center><FONT SIZE=8 COLOR=#futura>INDETERMINATE!</A></center>
<BR>
<center><FONT SIZE=6 COLOR=#FFFFFF>over the past five years I have presented
my images/language/design/signature to the global community via the world wide web.
a quantum leap from the humble beginnings of your intrepid author.
there is no comparison to the level of exposure available in this new medium.
what once was a wall, in a subway station on a deserted
platform is now a monitor in a young girls/boys bedroom.
here I am, in Bosnia, Brazil, Berlin and Bangkok.</A></center>
<BR>
<center><FONT SIZE=6 COLOR=#FFFFFF>in addition to my personal propaganda procedure:
I am giving respect and love to a tradition of imagined excellence.
those who were there know. those who were not, will always wonder.
life is relative to where you are: and what is happening around you.
but this can be changed. I am living proof.</A></center>
<BR>
<center><FONT SIZE=8 COLOR=#222222>because this is my story. and I own it.</A></center>
<BR>
<center><P><FONT SIZE=8 COLOR=#futura>
<A HREF="currently.htm" onMouseOver="window.status='SALMA';return true">
salma</A> </center>
<BR>
<BR>
<center><IMG SRC="fumefuk.gif"</center>
<BR>
<BR>
<center><P><FONT SIZE=11 COLOR=#66gg33>
<A H          tm" onMouseOver  window.status='dangerou    return true">
almost looks like I shot myself with the LOMO</A></FONT></center>
<BR>
<BR>
<BR>
<BR>
</body>
</html>
```

sixties

seventies

eighties

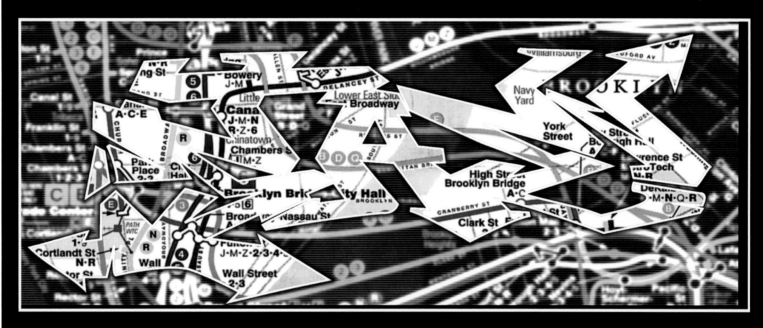

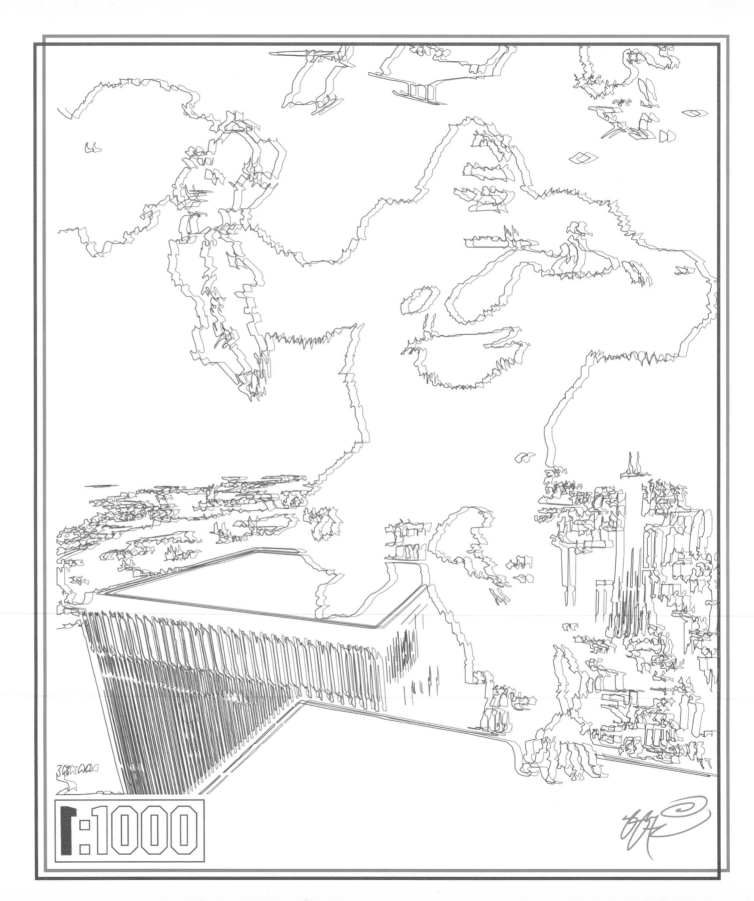

Г:1000

police&thieves.
you decide

stuck in houses big as mountains
people are trapped wondering
what life has in store for them
some of them find nothing
some of them find death
some just walk away to a better place

she shot me.
not once.
she shot from behind.
i couldn't see her
her soul was camouflaged.
i will bleed forever.

artoo, berlin 1999

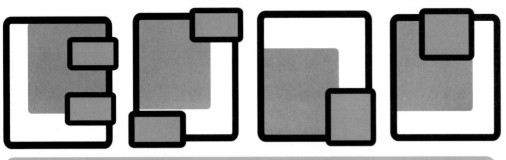

DAILY
OPERATION

NOW WITH OPAQUE INTENT

Queen gets the green, black sets you back

GOOD GAME

Lizzie Bag's
5 Finger
Discounts

ICE
GRILL

WHAT?!

NORTH PHILADELPHIA

TOYOTA CLUB

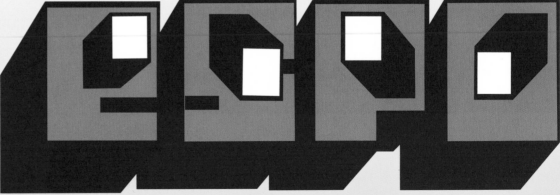

NO
DRAWING

but enough about you . . .

doing more for art and faith since 1985

stephen powers aka espo, new york 2000

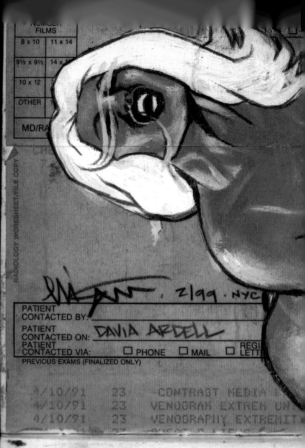

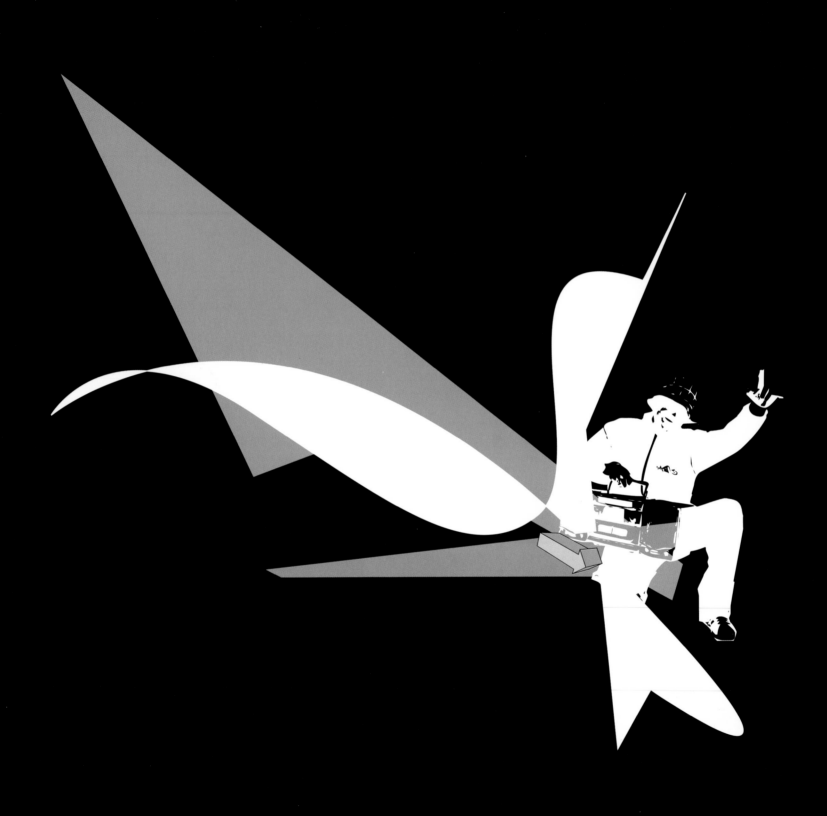

'can't live without my radio!', **lodownradio.com**

beach scene by **reas** aka todd james, new york 2000

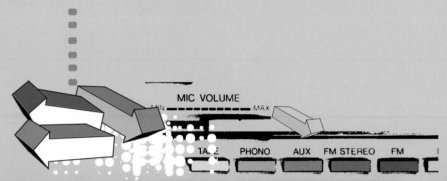

MIC VOLUME

MIN — MAX

TAPE   PHONO   AUX   FM STEREO   FM

feature break

the hiphop phenomenom
we got the **jazz**
headz digging deeper in your subconciousness
electronic warfare

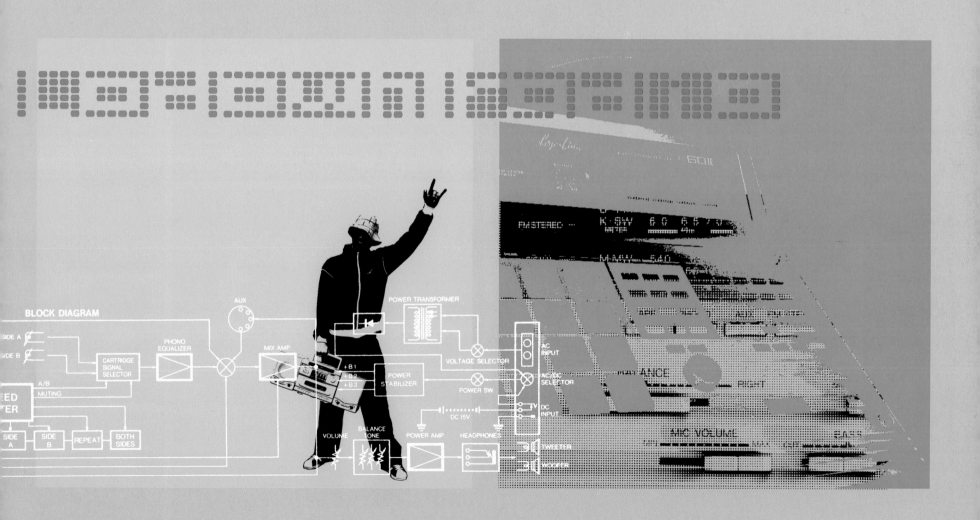

BLOCK DIAGRAM

SIDE A

SIDE B

CARTRIDGE
SIGNAL
SELECTOR

PHONO
EQUALIZER

AUX

MIX AMP.

POWER TRANSFORMER

POWER
STABILIZER

VOLTAGE SELECTOR

AC
INPUT

AC/DC
SELECTOR

POWER SW.

A/B

MUTING

ED
ER

+B1
+B2
+B3

TV DC
INPUT

SIDE
A

SIDE
B

REPEAT

BOTH
SIDES

VOLUME

BALANCE
TONE

DC 15V

POWER AMP.

HEADPHONE

TWEETER

WOOFER

lorec.
LODOWNRECORDINGS

goldie in the mix, photos supplied by ballard, a.d. and foley.
thanks to dc shoes.

skratchpiklz/beat junkiesTXT

on the wheelz of steel, part of the skratchpiklz in 1998.

198fourthousand **embolism** | high

antipop reco

FRESH
reagan era
mixtape revision
refractions

the antipop consortium, pictured by eddie otchere in 2000.

the mpc rebuild by critzla in 2000.

Recht hat er.

プシカろ☆

Sommer 1999

Tokyo. Sommer 1999

'kensei and bishop' design by **pact**

COltrane

How often within the inhuman traffic of one's
life span do you truly get to get'down&LO with a living legend?

Maybe once in a lifetime and they usually turn out to be decrepit old wrecks, burnt out
due to years of excess and overdoing it to death (bumping into Micheal Barrymore in
your local Tesco's doesn't really count now does it?) So when I got a seating ticket for
one of the don's yearly ubiquitous visit's to London's Ronnie Scott's, I got my mind in
line for - what turned out to be - one of the most intense Q&A'S I've ever conducted.
For a man in his 60's Roy Ayers rocks the mighty healthy demeanour playing the vibes
like he's making love.

THE MAN'S DEEP, FEEL HIS VIBRATIONS...

LD: You came up with the name 'Ubiquity' for your project and it's one of the most obviously
apt names for a band ever...

RA: "Well the name 'Ubiquity' means the state of being everywhere at the same time,
omniprescence. I used to tell people that I could be everywhere at the same time if everyone
had one of my albums at the same time."

LD: You've made some of the most legendary jazz fusion standards, and a lot of that music
came out of the 'Ubiquity' stable. What for you was the ultimate line-up, that you had?

RA: "It's hard to pick out what was the high or low moments, all the musicans who have
performed with me have been part of my ever growing career, but just about every group
I've had including my current group has high and low points. But the begining of my career
had a very spontaneous energy to it, the most unique time was from around 1975\76 up till
the "Sunshine" album."

LD: Those are your most played club moments and they're probably your most sampled
moments, but it seems you took a backseat role after that period, by not even appearing on
certain albums like Ubiquity's "Starbooty".

RA: "I think it happens to most artists, look at Stevie Wonder, you just come to the point
where you're doing so much, you take a break. But I'm always touring, I've been coming to
England every year since 1988, and even before that we were doing shows at the Hammersmith
Odeon with Tom Browne and Lonnie Liston Smith. Then I started playing Ronnie Scott's
every year, 'cause I really wanted to see what England was all about, because it's definitely
one of my major markets."

LD: Does having a market like this keep up your passion for music?

RA: "Yes, definitely. I'm mean, I'm into smooth jazz now, but my music has always been
smooth...."

LD: The again something like "We live in Brooklyn" had a darker vibe than the stuff you're
doing now, had more edge definitely...

RA: "Yeah well you know, a lot of people think I wrote 'We live in Brooklyn', but it was
actually a guy called Harry Whittaker that wrote the song, so a lot of people associate the
whole mood with me, but that was all down to Harry. He's a pianist who was with my group
in the early days and now he's with Roberta Flack.

LD: So who were your major influences in music?

RA: "Lionel Hampton, he was one of my idols. I look up to him. He gave me a set of vibe
mallets when I was five years old when I went to see him play. I always knew I was going to
be a musican, my mother used to say to me 'I'll see your name up in lights', and inspiration
like that gave me the motive to carry on."

vibin´ with the legend.

roy aYers

LD: How do you view a lot of the modern Jazz that's out at the moment?

RA: "I think there's a lot of guys out there that's Shuckin' and Jivin'...there's a lot of guys that are not smooth jazz artists, and a lot of so called smooth jazz stations out there play them. But if you remember guys like Wes Montgomery, Jimmy Smith or Ramsey Lewis, they all came out of the be-bop era but they were able to play a more commercially orientated music. I came from another school, which is like the school of Herbie Hancock and Lonnie Listen Smith. But you got all these guys who came along with JazzFunk or AcidJazzbut it's really just 'rinkydink'. And I'm talking about all these radio stations in America playing what is really just elevator music."

LD: So do you feel Jazz has totally lost its innovative edge?

RA: "They're using the name jazz, just because they can. The art of jazz is in the improvisation. You got cats putting some slick lines on their tracks, or using loops and calling it jazz. But it's the industry, they're trying to dictate how or what it should sound like. As an artist all I can do is to keep doing what I'm doing and the people see the difference. They can tell the bullshit from the realshit. I'm not saying who's real or who's not, let the people be the judge."

LD: What are your plans for 'Ubiquity 2000'?

RA: "2000? 2000Black (referring to one of his classic recordings). I just hope the blackman's mind can become more aware and more conscious of who he is, and what to do about his life and the presevation of self...and hope this Y2k don't kick all our ass. Hopefully everyone can be positive and radio starts using their influence and intelligence to play some real music. They should be playing Ray Gaskin(British keyboardist/vocalist and 'Ubiquity'member), they only play stuff like that in minimal spurts and they play these other guys and they ain't smooth or even jazz!"

LD: So you're not down with Acid Jazz?

RA: "I played Acid Jazz, I did all that. Do you remember Maiden Voyage? That's as smooth as you can get, even the vocal tracks like 'Sunshine' that's smooth, mellow, cool music. Yeah, I respect Acid Jazz, but the terminology came up like everything else...they said I was the Disco King, the Acid Jazz king. I swear I got articles saying this. All these terminologies come up, it's just pepertration of fraud. You got people with a beat, a loop it's not even about improvising and cats get away with it. It's unfortunate. Gilles Peterson came up with Acid Jazz, and now he doesn't even want to take credit for it (someone in the background mumbles something about Acid Jazz and Jamiroquai). Let me tell you about Jamiroquai, who I respect as an musican, or at least I did.Well my agent called me up and says "Well Roy I got you a gig with Jamiroquai, but his manager says Jamiroquai doesn't want you to do the show with him, 'cause he thinks you're too old.'I couldn't believe that."

LD: I can't believe the prat in the hat really said that. Can I put that in print?

RA: (looks me directly in the eye) "Oh man, it's the truth. I didn't do the gig. When my agent told me that I said 'How could he or his manager even say that? Doesn't he realize that someday if he lives to be 80 or 90 years old somebody's gonna turn round and say he's too old? C'mon, what's age got to do with it? You can't just cut off life like that."

LD: That's disrespect, he should be honoured to be playing on the same stage. If it wasn't for you cats, he'd have at least ten less artists to rip off.

RA: "You got to let life go on and be real or not speak on it at all. (In mocking voice) 'I don't want Ray Gaskin to play on my show, he's too young.' That was very discouraging for me to hear, I'm disappointed in him."

LD: So do you check for any of the new artists out there?

RA: "I'm in the stores all the time checking out and buying stuff. But I'm dissapointed in the record industry. They're cutting back and not promoting new music. They're scared of the internet,'cause it's taking power away from them, it's frightening to them. So they're only putting the push behind the sureshot guaranteed hitmakers. I'm just glad I've got my own record company and I'm putting out my own stuff now. To me, that's the name of the game, doing it for yourself. You've got to remember that all these big companies were once small, little people and that's the way to go."

LD: Do you ever see a point when you'll stop recording or touring?

RA: "I don't like to say, I'm happy to participate in the music for as long as possible.I want to continue playing Jazz. We're not like athletes who lose their powers as they grow older, music is different. If you take care of yourself you can play for as long as you live. Look at Miles Davis or Dizzy Gillespie, those cats played till they died, which is a great way to go out."

LD: Aight, first I wanna know what "NIA" stands for.
B: It is one of the seven principles of our belief-system. In America, we have an african american holiday called "Kwaanza". And "NIA" is for purpose.
The whole concept behind "NIA" is realizing your purpose through struggle, you go through life´s struggles and you realize who you are. It´s that universal struggle that everybody goes through. It´s there in good times as well, but the struggle part is what makes your soul what it is. Especially now, facing the millenium and all that, as we, the people, are faced with so many messages that overwhelm us. There´s never been a point in history when people had access to so much information. You walk out your house and you see all those billboards that read "Buy this, eat this, watch this" and subconsciously, you take all that stuff in. So it´s really important to maintain your sense of self, whether you´re a rapper, a graff writer or a computer programmer, whatever your passion in life is.
Well, as we said the new album is called "NIA". For us, it´s personal, because we went through a lot of experiences making this album. That´s what made us call the album "NIA", as we went through a lot of personal struggles, struggles as artists. It´s us standing there and saying, "This is us, this is what God has revealed to us. This is

own way.
LD: You´re also involved with Quannum Spectrum?
B: Yeah, Quannum, that´s our crew. We started the label called Solesides. In 1997, we shut down the label to move on to something bigger and stronger. So, in the beginning of ´98, we gave birth to Quannum. The first release was the Quannum Spectrum album, and by this we wanted to give you a little glimpse at what everybody´s doing, from us to Latyrx to Shadow and so on.
We all live in the Bay Area, San Francisco. We like to refer to what we call the "earth renaissance" of independent hip hop, which took place in the Bay Area, respectively the West Coast and took off with Too Short, DigitalUnderground being the second, on with the Pharcyde, the Hieroglyphics, Hobo Junction in ´92/´93... can´t forget Freestyle Fellowship, the pioneers, you know.
 Now it´s Jurassic 5, Dilated Peoples down south and up north you got people like Rasco, Planet Asia, Encore, Hieros, us... and so on. There´s a certain movement going on in Cali, and that´s a dope thang.
LD: J5 and Black Eyed Peas told me they were getting a lot more airplay over here in Europe than in the States.
B: I think it´s turning around right now because the Jurassic album is gonna get a lot of love, Dilated are getting much love, Defari is getting love...

it seems to be moving in cycles. Things seem to be standing still, and all of a sudden, Baamm!! In the mainstream it´s like "Where is that coming from?", but it´s always been there. Back to the days in ´88, when De La released "3 ft high and rising", through late ´89, early ´90 when Brand Nubian and Leaders of the New School came out. People was like "Wow, what is this?" It is moving in cycles but that´s what keeps this hip hop thing alive: The ability to reinvent itself at the drop of a dime. With us, we´re only trying to make good, pure hip hop. If only 30,000 people buy this record in the States, that´s a success to us, you know, we can eat. If one million buy this record, that´s cool as well. I mean the goal of any artist is to have his music heard and get appreciated especially when it´s genuine and has integrity. I feel like we make music that crosses all boundaries of race, age, creed, sex... everything. Basically, we have a chemistry and we have the ability to make universal music, something that we would want to hear. Bottom line.

blackalicious blackalicious blackalicious blackalicious blackalicious blackalicious blackalicious blackalicious blackalicious blackalicious blackalicious blackalicious blackalicious

SOULS OF MISCHIEF

we represent
the underground mc.
a plus, opio
tajai & phesto d.

people under the stairs

"The wackest thing an MC can do is not to be himself and not to express himself. So many MCs try to express a character, they are just actors and when they leave the studio they get back to being themselves."

Turntable driven hip hop music has grown massively in the last few years, and everywhere, from New York to London, and from Berlin to Tokyo new crews rise from the underground. One of San Franciscos most promising acts for thefuture is the dynamic duo of Thes One and Double K, also known as People Under The Stairs. The two met several years back when they were digging the crates in the downtown record store "Martin's Records", and in hindsight Thes One believes that the meeting was meant to happen. "We kind of looked at each other like 'Aight, you are the guy that I heard about, you are the guy that makes these beats'. We hooked up and it all worked out, and now when we get in the studio it's like one person, not like a crew." Rooted deeply in the consciousness and culture of the westcoast's underground hip hop scene, their first album is a well crafted beat manifesto, that lives of its 60s and 70s jazz-rock and funk samples, truly original and funny song intros and lyrics that take you on a ride through the minds of two real hip hop connoisseurs.

"I'm tired of hearing MCs going on about how clever and hard they are. I'm tired of that, it just gets so old. For me the wackest thing an MC can do is not to be himself and not to express himself.," Thes One stresses. "It's the same with the beats. We try to dig away from the trends, we try to hunt down the more obscure stuff, the independent artists from that era, because we are independent hip hop artists from this era and it is fun to go back and find people who were putting the records out by themselves back in that era." Despite the fact that People Under The Stairs have paid their dues by rocking underground shows at colleges and universities and playing as support act for the likes of the Roots, Ugly Duckling, the Alkoholiks and Defari, the response to their album in the States, but particularly in LA, has been really bad. In a time where pretty Puff Daddy jigginess is en vogue amongst LA's multi racial hip pop community real headz like Thes One and Double K don't have an easy position. "It seemed to me the further we got from LA, the better the reception was. The West Coast for the best part wasn't feeling it at all, and we almost gave up. For a couple of months we were just laying off, but once the album got overseas, it sparked new hope. In Europe I have noticed that people see it as an advantage (to be different), and that's the way it should be in hip hop. If you don't sound like everyone else and come with some original stuff, you should get some respect."

eddie otchere
presents
BODY & SOUL

SHEETS
9½ × 12 inch

store in a safe and cool place

PHOTO IND. CO., LTD.   LONDON, UK

common ground
underground dwellers

crooked eye aka iron lounge aka hot nickelz aka johnny blaze aka mr. tical... if can' say it all, just say meth!
jeru tha damaja, true from the heart!

eddie otchere
presents

SHEETS
9¼ × 12 inch

BODY&SOUL

store in a safe and cool place

PHOTO IND. CO., LTD.

LONDON, UK

allen iverson
common sense points out
rza as bobby digital soon to be sweated by robbie analog

ME AND

CRY FREEDOM

A conversation between Dead Prez and Yinka Oyewole, Fotos by Angela Boatwright

A couple of months ago during my weekly dose of Yo MTV Raps, a video suddenly stuck out like the proverbial sore thumb among the usual iced-out, booty shaking celluloid. What marked out this three and a half minutes was not state of the art computer generated graphics, breathtaking locations or stunning camera work, indeed it looked like the video with the lowest budget. No, it was its impact, energy and complete lack of resemblance to anything else on that show. The video for "Hip-Hop", the lead single off Dead Prez's debut album Let's Get Free, commences with a gratuitous up close booty shot which draws you in then a banner flashes: "NOW THAT WE'VE GOT YOUR ATTENTION!" An army of rowdy black men with their faces obscured by bandanas attacks you through the screen. Two highly animated, dreadlocked brothers, wielding megaphones are conducting

a crowd of black people in a claustrophobically small hall! I Ching symbols; more banners - Discipline, Strength, etc; perfectly choreographed Martial Arts groups; hugely afroed black women hold their fists in the air. But this is no retrospective on the Civil Rights, it is a Rap video at the end of 1999. Unsurprisingly the video was banned from US television screens. Its very existence in this post PE's Fight The Power, nihilistic, "I want it all now" age almost beggars belief. But beware this might just be the first droplet of water in the wave of the turning tide. I met both halves of the DPs: Stic and M1, at Loud's NY offices and immediately noticed how relaxed and unpretentious they are. Stic leans back in his chair, M1 listens intently. M1 asks me where I'm from and my heritage. Stic asks the meaning of my name. They both extend hospitality more akin to a reunion between distant relatives than an interview between strangers. I have a pair of fine sistas with me to take photographs, whom these guys treat with great respect. I already sense these aren't average rap cats…

Caught up in the mix an shit, an I ain't trying hear shit, dun my crew got cash to get, splash with the pistol if I have to…" - from "Pistol"

So first off how old are you guys, where are you from and what are your musical influences?
Stic: "I'm 25, and was born and raised Tallahassee, Florida. I grew up listening to blues like Bobby Blue Bland."
M1: "I'm 27, I was born in Jamaica, came up in NYC. My mum was a jazz singer so I love Ella Fitzgerald and Billie Holiday and of course I love reggae."
So how did you guys get into rapping?
M1: "Well Hip Hop always been there for me, whether it's rapping or whatever!"
Stic: "One of my peoples was a DJ, he used to spin records at parties and I used to go along and check him out. I wanted to deejay as well but he was like, no man you should emcee, so I got into that! "
So how did you hook up?
M1: "I ain't gonna front, I got peeps that's incarcerated. I got involved in some bad drug situations but I knew there was something more. So I went to Florida. I didn't know about going to college or nothing but I managed to get in Florida A&M University. I knew I was looking for something and that turned out to be Stic who wasn't even in school at the time."
Stic: "Well I came up in the usual shit, there was a lot of crack around, a lot of stupid shit, it was the autobiography of Malcolm X that opened my mind."
So what do you think of the state of Hip Hop right now?
Stic: "Hip Hop is a reflection of the state of the world. Get money! That's the message pushed at people. That's why niggas call themselves Capone this and Scarface that. But life's bigger than that! We've got to address our basic needs!"
So what's the name about?
Stic: "Dead prez is an abbreviation of dead presidents - those little pieces of paper you need to eat."
M1: "Greenbacks, you know, It's a slang term. And it caught on real fast once it came out - like the word nigga. Everybody was like I gotta have dead presidents!"
Stic: "But we flipping the meaning around cos they the bloodsuckers of the poor. So we're saying dead the president "

"…I'm an African an' know what's happening…"- from "African"

So do you have a message?
M1: " Not specifically. We're not preaching, we're talking about power and freedom. We want overthrow our oppressors, break our chains."

Stic: "
When you talk
about white power or the
capitalist structure that evolved out
of white supremacy controlling things, people say you´re racist.
But we're not talking about people being devils or outer-space conspiracy theories and all that craziness. We´re talking about reality!"
M1: " It's like the even in the USA itself, when white people came they wiped out the indigenous peoples. It ain't no secret!
So who are you talking to, who is your music for?
Stic: "Poor and oppressed people across the world."
M1: "But particularly for Africans. That's why I call myself an African, not cos I've been there but wherever we are that's what black people are. Whether you in the UK, USA or the Caribbean. I was born in Jamaica and raised in New York but I don't claim none of that - I'm African. It's a fact that Europeans formulated capitalism, which oppresses people from slavery to colonialism to now. It ain't right for any people to starve, have poor education or a high infant mortality rate. It ain't right that they eat four times as much as us. So it's in their best interest to listen."
So what's the album about?

Stic: "Straight up slave rebellion!"

"…A Nigga like me don't playa hate I just stay awake…"- from "Hip-Hop"

So you're not dissing certain rappers with the "Get Money" mentality?
M1: " Hell no. Jay-Z man, that's my brother!"
Stic: " But don't get it wrong. Let me use an analogy. If I got people, family in the military and the shit comes down that could be my brother but in the struggle you're either for our freedom or against it. If you're against it you gotta go!"
You mention people like Master P in your lyrics; him and Jay-Z are selling a lot of records so obviously people are paying attention. How do you hope to get your heard?
Stic: "People listen to it cos Master P can backup what he says with the money

he has. So we need to back up what we say with what we do! So if I talk about being healthy then I've gotta live healthy - cos if I'm not gonna do push ups and not eat meat then why should you! If we talking about food, clothes and shelter - then we gotta have clothing drives, food drops!"
M1: "Yeah rapping can´t really change anything but it can make people aware. In the movement I'm involved with we sell a paper called the Burning Spear in train stations, we call them train runs. I do that like 3 or 4 times a week for a couple hours each time - but that's not as much as I would like and I do feel a conflict. "
So what is your goal - where do you wanna be in five years?
Stic:" I wanna be free yo!"
What is freedom?
Stic: "That's a good question - I don't have all the answers. To me self-determination is the highest part of democracy and that's freedom. You gotta be in control of your own shit. We need to be able to defend that whether with intellect or an AK."
M1: "It's about control over your own destiny and being able to protect that, to do that you need an army."
Stic: "We gotta take care of the community. If you need a shirt, we've got to be able to make it, so we need skills. I'm learning to sew so I can make dashikis. But we're not saying you should only have so much - you just shouldn't be taking from others to get it. We should be billionaires - not necessarily in wealth but in what we produce."

M1: "We are such a productive people."
What do you think of the Internet?
M1: "It's just another hype."
Stic: "It's another thing for you to spend money on building up their system. People say history goes in cycles, but like my man M1 says, history goes in spirals so shit comes back around but it's not exactly the same. So the Internet's not really new, it's just a continuation of what's come before - it's more communications."
M1: "It's like when phones first came out, everyone didn't have a phone. People used to go to the person in they neighbourhood who had a phone and use theirs so just cos they say "Oh here's the Internet", it's not like everyone has access it."
Stic: "You know black folks in the ghetto can't afford computers, we still just trying to stay alive."
I mean the question in terms of people like Public Enemy releasing tracks over the Internet, they say it's a tool for independence.
Stic: "If you can use it as a tool, that's cool. But I look at it this way: On a plantation you got a part were the plants grow, where the dogs stay, etc. So if they say here's the Internet you gotta realise you´re still on the plantation. It might be a different part of the plantation but it's still all the plantation."
Is there anything else you'd like to say to the peeps?
Stic: "Yeah, we can learn. We can all learn."

There's something very traditionally African about the DPs, something almost timeless - a vibe you'll find in the South, in blues and jazz, something Bob Marley, Peter Tosh and Fela Kuti all personified. They want peace and justice, they say they'll bust guns to get it, just like gangsters will bust guns to get paper. There's a lesson here for those who want to listen, in Dead Prez's own words: "We can all learn" and we need to…

IMAGES IN A DIFFERENT LIGHT
photographics by angela boatwright

start left:
amel larrieux contemplating,
the roots live double exposed over the 52X,
2/3 of missin' linx and ghostwriter,
fat joe, cuban link and son,
ja rule and daughter brittney

photographics by angela boatwright

start left:
lil' kim filming for mtv's fanatic,
redman and keith murray on the defjam rooftop in 1997

photographics by angela boatwright

peter smolik being a brat getting his hair braided

13

intro:

lodown is still boarding, thrills & entertainment.
das soziologische profil des zeitungseinräumers ist äußerst wichtig, daher die kleine untertiteländerung auf dem cover.
ansonsten wünschen wir viel spaß bei der visuellen defragmentierung und anschließender informationsexploitation dieser publikation.

in order of appearance
covershot is pat duffy frontsideflipping a fake rooftop in cologne by flach
the intro you starring at is chad muska, blunt transfer in l.a., shot by thomas campbell, above the lately discovered radio rahim blaster in eastberlin shot by mrk.

chad´s no stranger to makeshift fun
tired of skating the same ol´ bench shit
in venice beach, chad gets some help from the
next construction site in form of some chipboards
and utilises them as launchpad an runway on the
unskateble rooftops to bridge a gap no one else flipped over before. the muska gap, still alive on your playstation.
...tired of skating the same ol´ gap he throws some kickflip fakies on his makeshift skatepark bank.
lack of power has no meaning for chad as long as his omnipresent blaster is boostin´ them fat beats.
foley was first on the kniper

classic cityshots by alexis zavialoff
urban atheletes exploiting the worlds capitals

aaron suski fs nosebluntslide, soho, nyc 1997

opposite page:
**williamsburgbridge asylum, brooklyn,
mike wright fs 180 nosegrind, new york 1997**

clockwise this page:
**mike connolly buttcrackollie in brooklyn,
ian reid, videodocumentary for the next eastern exposure,
paul leung in unfriendly environment, ollie to a platform,
dan zimmer loungin',
john carter ollie nightshift,
you just gotta' love him, harold hunter in a car hustle, all nyc 1997**

opposite page:
spencer fujimoto in a fs crooked to fakie manner, nyc 1997

rodney torres and geovanne moya flushing on mainstreet, nyc 1998

opposite page far right:
rodney torres, backside five-o to revert

massive pic
bombardement

LODOWN NO.23 FREE FORM

aaron suski fiftyfifties a lexus wreck in queens

PLUS **GRAPHICAL OVERLOAD**
ALL COMIN' THROUGH IN OCT.2000
NEW AND IMPROVED

BE DANGEROUS
Drive
Desperate

Watcha lookin my way? Faggot BITER
LO DOWN
INSTRUCTIONAL MATERIALS
CHICAGO, ILLINOIS 60601

grahics by **honza**, pfadfinderei mitte, berlin 1999

grahics by **critzla**, pfadfinderei mitte, berlin 1999

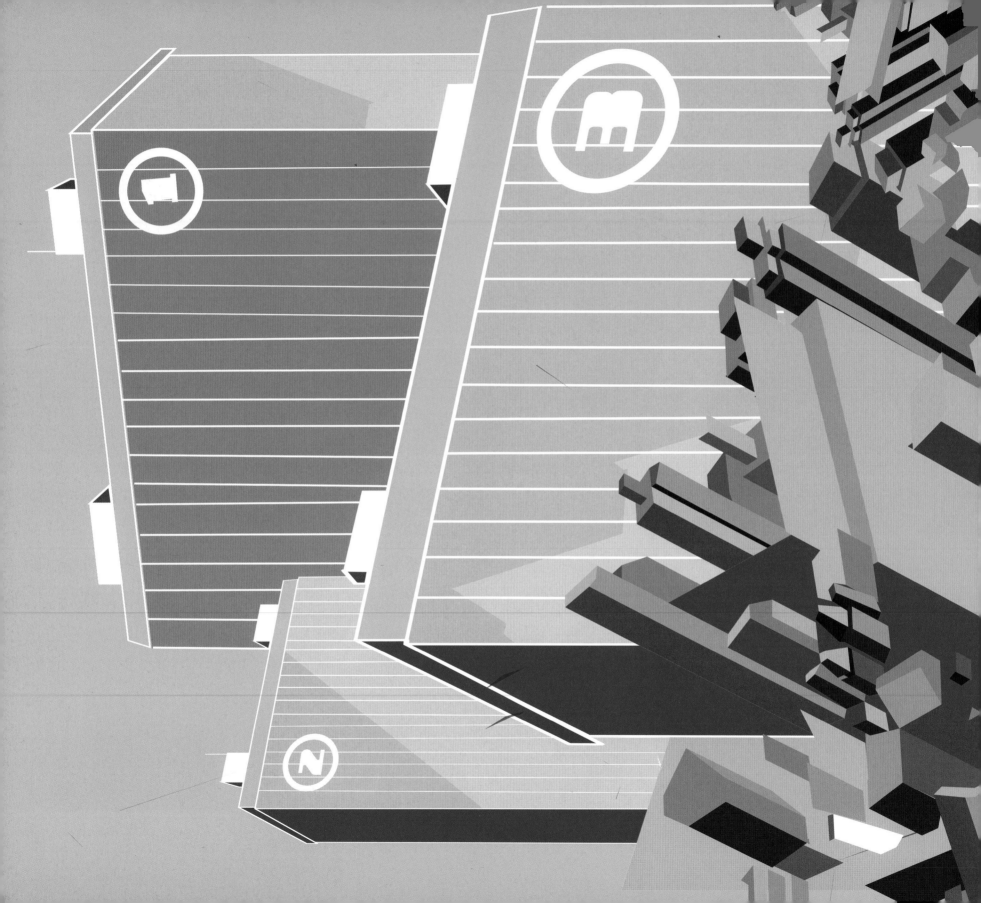

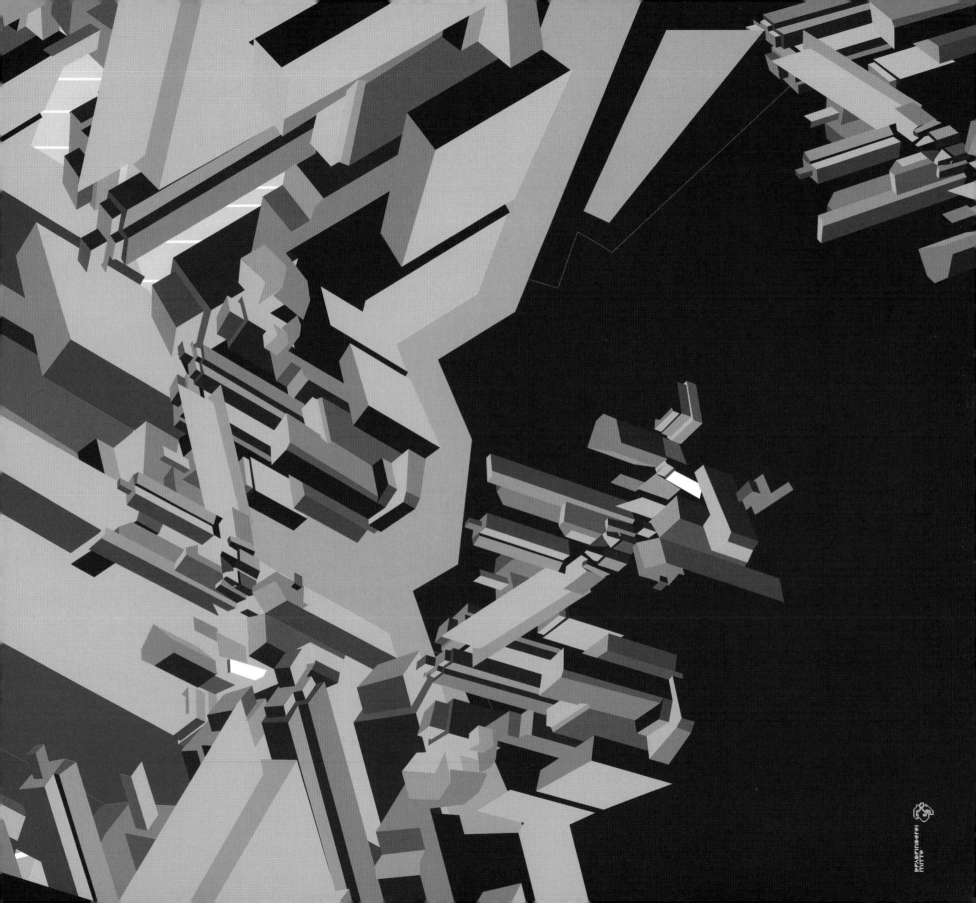

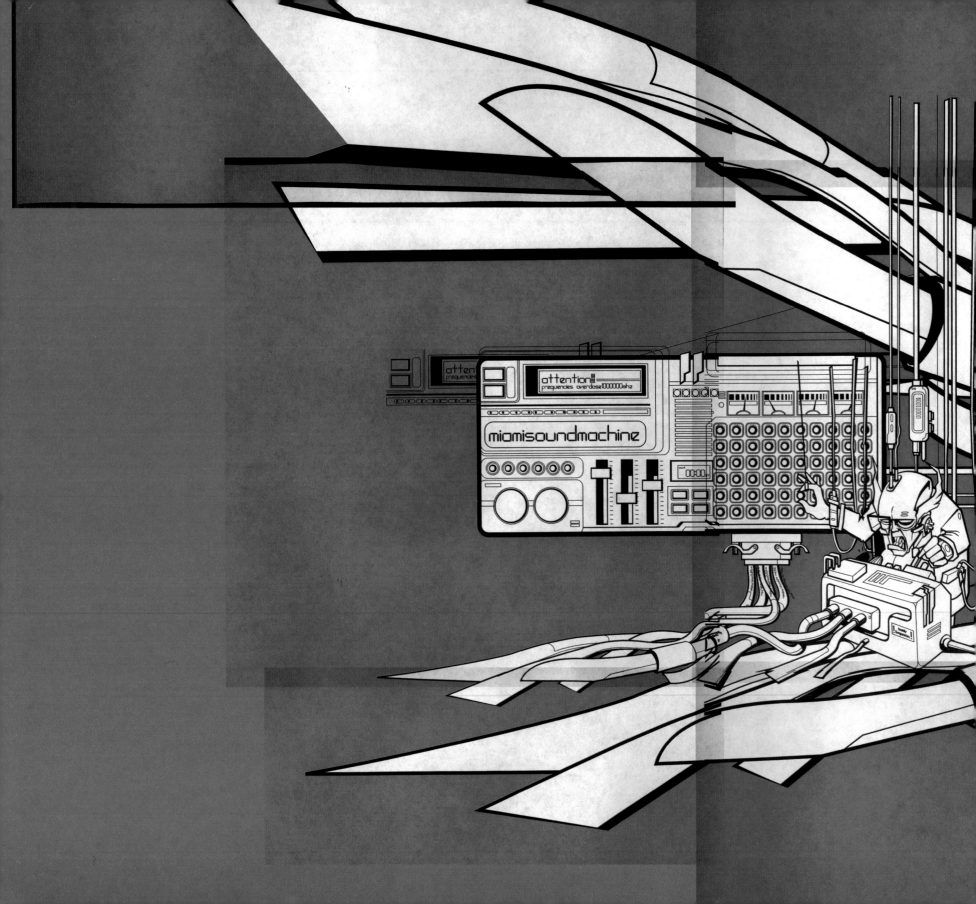

grahics by **pact**, leipzig 1999

Jake Mandell is in the process of establishing himself as a landmark in a vast, bleak electronic landscape. With a whole host of releases already under his belt on more labels than you'd care to mention Jake is coming of age, gone are the days of "Parallel Processes" which marked his breakthrough a few years ago. Now Jake is learned in the art of electronic tomfoolery and over the past months has been exploring new avenues. A recent tour in Germany saw Jake displeasing the IDM purists with straight techno and a release on "Force Inc" threw a great big spanner in the works for all the electronic mailing list kiddies. Jake refuses, however, to bow to any trend and he is content with appealing to a diverse audience, be it experimental, techno or electronica. How such a track record came about is a very complex issue and ratherthan carry on we'll let Jake explain that himself..........

I have a secret that I have been ashamed of until now. I can't remember how many times I have been too embarrased to name my crushes, from that girl in third grade to whom I always lent my crayons, to the mysterious redhead that passed me on the bus yesterday. But I'd like to break open the barriers that have been churning nervously in my stomach for the past twelve years. I'm going to admit my crush, even if she squeals and tells the teacher. Ready?

I'm in love with computers. I didn't know what to call the feelings when I first met her when I was thirteen, her 2-bit graphics and squawky beeps both enrapturing and exotic. Nor do I know what brought about this revelation. But now that I shared with you my most tender, pinkest secret, let me explain a bit.

The once-intimate relationship between an artist and his or her tools has entered a dark age that began when artists started using computers. The immediate simplicity of holding a weathered brush in your hands and stirring tubes of oil paints with your thumb cannot be easily emulated through the abstract remove of a mouse and a monitor. In the familiar artist-brush, writer-pen, or musician-instrument relationships, the tools become part of a physical relationship that involves fetishism and affection. Every artist cradles a favorite brush, every writer grasps a lucky pen, and wonderful instruments are treasured throughout centuries. It's possible to renew these lost bonds between creativity and tools of creation, even when using a computer to create. What we're missing is love.

After many frustrating years writing computer music, I realized that in order for my music to have the emotional and physical impact that I was hearing in my head, I would have to learn to let my love for machines escape its tempestuous confinement. At first I thought this would be difficult. Isn't showing (and even worse, admitting!) love for a computer tantamount to decrying humanity? Just the opposite! The idea of half a century of collaboration, of people from across the globe sharing resources, ideas, and tools to create a magnificent paradigm of human accomplishment is indeed lustful. A computer is not just an extension of humanity, but the very embodiment of humanity. We love ideas. A nun claims marriage to a specter. A monk devotes his life to the exacting study of superstition. And I write music based on three generations of human achievement.

Now the computer beckons with pouty lips whenever I have a creative urge. My music was transformed once I realized that I was amazed by my instrument. Instead of wrestling with awkward interfaces, buggy software, and jerky mice, I now revel in one of our most enlightened accomplishments. Even though I risk being called a social outcast, I can't help but admit it.

I am in love.

Inspired by humanity, driven by love, executed on our brightest invention, here are fifteen love songs about one of the most complex relationships in human history. Voices are grafted onto circuits, melodies are sutured to mathematically shifting timbres. Humano-robotic rhythms dance gently with organometallic modulations. Jake Mandell's third album, Love Songs for Machines, will be available December 2000 from Carpark Records.

Jake Mandell

Love Songs for Machines

Does the language of violence sometimes appear to you as complex as the Morse code? As network of misuse of power and intrigues in an impenetrable jungle? Are you perhaps searching for an idol? Help yourself and decode the mistery of the bad boys and mass murderers. Lay back and enjoy the riddle. Make use of your knowledge and have fun of course. Here it turns out who really exposes the faces of doom.

PACT PRESENTS

DICTATOR QUESTION
PRIZE WINNING GAME

Find ten famous considerable) dictators and power-hungry criminals of the present or the past among the illustrations on the right side! Assign these dictators to the correct name! But pay attention! Not all of them are already dictators or criminals and will not become as such! Write down the names (first name, surname) of the ten dictators on a post paid postcard and send it in until july 7th 2001 (date as postmark) to: **Pact. Dieskaustrasse 155, 04249 Leipzig, Germany** or send an email to: **Dictator@pact-net.de** Do you know the correct answers? You can win 20 original drawings of members of the pact organisation.

DROPPED INTO THIS WORLD, HE WAS A BIT MIXED-UP.

contributers to
schizophrenic.

skism
artoo
a.d.camera
kinsey
futura
stash
twist
pact
alexis zavaloff
eddie otchere
thomas campbell
steff plaetz
angela boatwright
graphic havoc
jest & alife
kostas seremites
site
espo
kr
rostarr
mark gonzales
eli gesner and zooyork
shepard fairey
scott snyder
chris glanz
ssurplus
gio estevez
pfadfinderei mitte
ricky powell

and of course
foley and marok

mad props to.
marley
hesse
steffanie
martin
& goetz

and the onlinestaff

visual sound bombing

STEREOTYPE

CONTROL FOR .00
and beyond

SCHIZOPHRENIC CONTROL

WWW.LODOWN.COM

ldwn camp headquarters.
lützowstrasse 68
10785 berlin/germany

tel. +49 265 2096 / fax. +49 265 1982
info@lodown.de

schizophrenic@lodown.com
marok@lodown.com

thanks to all support and love we got for the project 'lodown'!

please turn off the light, foley!